What People Are Saying

"What truly sets this book apart is its perspective on continuous growth. It goes beyond surface-level productivity tips, encouraging readers to view each moment as an opportunity to learn and evolve. Reading this book felt like a refreshing reminder that nothing is out of reach. This book is a must-read if you're ready to turn your moments into meaningful progress."

– Neal Sneller, Executive Director
Prescott Meals on Wheels
https://prescottmealsonwheels.org

I0558715

***

"The Magic of a Moment is a fable that resonates with pre-teens, teens, and adults alike, teaching the essentials of organization, personal productivity, and growth. Readers of all ages will be inspired by Mr. Mac's strategies and his willingness to mentor and celebrate the success of others."

– Janene Panfil, sister, wife, mom, grandmother, leader,
and a woman striving to live her best life
with her family and friends

***

"I loved this book! At times, Phil Knight, Joe Dispenza, Stephen Covey, and Eckhart Tolle…not copying but pulling from and adding to these ideas in a way that makes personal growth accessible. I'd encourage everyone in my life to read this and apply these seven concepts."

– Eric Groves, Vice President
Liaison International
https://www.liaisonedu.com

***

"The power of The Magic of a Moment *is one of the best tools in your time management/self-help toolbox that a person can begin to utilize! Everyone should have opportunity to learn these 'assignments' as early as possible to make the most of the magic in all of their life's moments!"*

– Neal Tessmann, Retired Basketball Coach
Embry-Riddle Aeronautical University
https://erau.edu

***

"This book details a simple and practical way to apply specific tools for turning 'intention' into 'accomplishment' and capturing the value of every moment along the way."

– Robbie Nicol, Retired Healthcare Executive

***

"This book beautifully intertwines life lessons with a heartfelt narrative, drawing readers into the personal experiences of the protagonist. The author skillfully blends wisdom into the story, making the lessons comprehensible and meaningful. Enjoyable book to read."

– Marie Larson, Real Estate Agent
https://marielarson.com

***

"This book explores a story and the power of relationships that connect you with concepts, activities to improve your life and performance, and the value and purpose of daily intentions to achieve results."

– Dr. Jim Hundrieser, Senior Advisor to the President
National Association of College and University Business Officers
Nacubo.org

***

"Thoughtful, encouraging, helpful, and kind."

– Richard Ach, Civic Leader and Philanthropist

The Magic of a Moment

UNLOCK THE POTENTIAL IN EVERY MOMENT

Gary L. Fretwell

The Magic of a Moment
Unlock the Potential in Every Moment

RHG Media Productions
21519 Knoll Way,
Castro Valley, CA 94546

ISBN 979-8-9919467-0-4 (paperback)
ISBN 979-8-9919467-1-1 (hardcover)
ISBN 979-8-9919467-2-8 (ebook)

Visit us online at www.YourPurposeDrivenPractice.com
Printed in the United States of America.

Dedication

My sincere thanks and love to my incredible wife, Nancy, for being my rock and cheerleader throughout the writing journey of this book. She believed in me and the beauty of every magical moment life offers. Let's cherish each moment together!

Acknowledgments

So many have contributed to my beliefs, thoughts, and perspectives on making the most of life.

My wife encouraged me along this journey to write my thoughts and share those things I believe to have had the most impact on the course of my life. This book would not have been possible without her endless support.

My brothers and children were wonderfully supportive of my efforts to write my ideas down in this book. I especially want to thank Tristan for his very constructive editorial recommendations.

During my career, I had the opportunity to work with many very impressive colleagues. When I shared my ideas and the thoughts I was capturing in *The Magic of a Moment*, they were so helpful and encouraging. This was also true for many of my friends when I shared the concept.

I've been a lifelong learner. I have read, listened to, or attended training on many of these concepts. In recent years, this has included many amazing podcasters.

I will not be able to name all the great minds I have drawn from, but I do want to name a few.

David Allen changed how I looked at personal productivity and gave a fantastic paradigm, which, like many others, changed my life.

James Clear wrote *Atomic Habits*, which states the importance of the habits we incorporate into our lives. His focus on becoming what you want to be was important in my thinking.

All Abdalla continually provides invaluable content on productivity, culminating in his book *Feel Good Productivity*.

Like me, Dr. Ben Carson came from humble beginnings but found an entire world in books. How we start isn't important, but what we do with our lives.

Tony Robbins's speeches and programs were inspirational to me. He helped me realize the amazing potential all of us have.

Elon Musk is known for his innovations, but his approach to each day, making the most of every moment, truly inspires me.

Finally, I think of someone everyone knows but I have never met, Theodore Roosevelt. All my friends and colleagues know how much I think of his accomplishments and how he lived his life. I have read every book I can about him and, to this day, frequently go back to them. One of his most famous quotes truly captures the way I look at life and what I hope *The Magic of a Moment* will inspire in others. He said, "It is not the critic who counts; not the man who points out how the strong man stumbles or where the doer of deeds could have done them better. The credit belongs to the man who is actually in the arena, whose face is marred by dust and sweat and blood; who strives valiantly; who errs, who comes short again and again, because there is no effort without error and shortcoming; but who does actually strive to do the deeds; who knows great enthusiasms, the great devotions; who spends himself in a worthy cause; who at the best knows in the end the triumph of high achievement, and who at the worst, if he fails, at least fails while daring greatly, so that his place shall never be with those cold and timid souls who neither know victory nor defeat."

These great minds have given me and many others so much. The writing of this book is the result of all of the learning, inspiration, and support I have received from all of them.

Contents

1

Who is Josh Douglas?

Like many auditoriums, Mcallister Auditorium has still, musty air. The vast hall remains eerily quiet in the mid-morning. Dust dances on the streams of light that pierce through the small windows over the balcony. If you allow yourself and listen closely, the old structure seems to groan with age and time spent either empty or full.

With a moment's pause, one can almost hear the echoes of musicals, dancers gliding across the stage, and numerous speakers conveying their messages. It all echoes through the empty building. The history, the uncounted events, and the people who have now visited McAllister are all but memories, forgotten ones. The grand, old hall is empty now and seems a waste deserted like this. Peter Hamilton walks through its empty aisles toward the stage as he ponders the announcement this evening and the many people who will file in to hear from Josh Douglas.

Peter, a ten-year veteran reporter from the *Wall Street Journal*, arrived in New Orleans late last night. His task is to interview the newest business flavor of the moment, the "sensational" Josh Douglas. Peter's experience with these "phenomenon" caused him to bristle at the thought of another interview like this. Peter had seen too many of these types of "shooting stars." Too often, these stars often fade fast or end up leaving their office in handcuffs.

Yet, Josh's fresh face demanded the attention he now received. Peter had worked hard to set up this meeting with Josh Douglas' assistant over the past three weeks after the news was that there was to be a significant announcement made today here in New Orleans.

Peter had done his homework on Josh and felt confident in his knowledge of this "wonder boy." Through his research, he knew Josh Douglas founded Generation One when only twenty-seven, which now, ten years later, emerged as the trailblazer in the emerging field of nanotechnology. Out of nowhere, the company established itself as the leader in this highly competitive field in a short amount of time. Josh's young company catapulted past other more established companies and now consistently outperformed everyone. It was a juggernaut that ruthlessly focused on creating the industry's leader in this field.

As Peter walked down the tile floor of the auditorium aisle, his footsteps reverberated off the walls. He made steady but noisy progress toward the interview, which will take place in a small room in the back of the auditorium. As he walked, Peter wondered how it was possible that at thirty-seven years old, Josh had legitimately achieved so many remarkable results. What was the secret of his success, and how is it possible? After many years of interviewing and getting to know business leaders, Peter was skeptical about anyone's ability to go from nothing to such significant accomplishments.

Peter's experience suggested shortcuts were often taken, some of which were illegal or unethical. He thought to himself. I can't let my cynicism get in the way of this interview. It would help if you were as objective as possible.

One thing was clear: in a relatively short time, Generation One had created some of the most solid and innovative advances possible in a field that takes no prisoners. Peter thought, can it be only in the past ten years that such significant innovation and development could occur? Could this happen legitimately? Peter thought and was convinced, "No way, shortcuts must have been taken." There must be something that can be uncovered which will explain the company's uncanny success.

As Peter walked past the stage, he mused that it was entirely unexpected and unprecedented for any leader so young to emerge from relative obscurity, much less have such achievements.

However, Josh Douglas had done just that and was now the toast of the business world. Yet, he remained an enigma to many. Since creating the company, he and his young team have made seemingly unstoppable progress. Sure, they had all of the typical issues and concerns of a start-up, but regardless of the competition or the market pressures, the company had continued its march to the top of the field. In his presentation, four hours from now, Josh will announce that Generation One will go public and surely will be one of the most anticipated public offerings ever. Not only will this make Josh and his team extremely rich, but it will also make him one of the elite business leaders in the world.

As Josh waited for Peter to arrive, he sat in the small holding room, totally unaffected by the pending announcement.

Instead, he quietly continued his work on some notes that he had put in a tattered old folio. He thought having these moments and an opportunity to think was a treat. "No time like the present to begin work on the future." While waiting for his announcement and interview with Peter, Josh quietly reflected on his company and felt satisfied with its progress, and at the same time, a rush of thoughts on what to do next came to mind. The small, windowless room provided a conducive atmosphere for contemplating the future.

It makes sense to use the time before the interview with Peter Hamilton. He should be here at any moment, and then the discussion on how, why, and what you have done differently would begin. If only he and his readers knew how simple it is, he thought, it's something all of us could do.

Josh shifted his attention as he waited and began to jot down thoughts that came to him that he would include in his presentation. As always, as the idea came to him, he quickly captured them. Josh knew his audience tonight would want to learn more about the future direction of his company, so he added some notes on what to include, but at the same time, he only wanted to say a little. Josh was still deciding whether announcing some of these ideas tonight was wise, but regardless, he tried to capture them.

People often make observations about Josh: he always seemed to have something going on. He always seemed to be doing something regardless of when you saw him, yet he never seemed stressed, pressured, or over-whelmed. Quiet progress seemed to mark his days, and his colleagues and competitors constantly noted him. Today was no different than any other. Even alone, waiting for his pivotal presentation, his thoughts flowed as he continued writing. Some had said his folio was like a second brain. It's strange for someone in such a high-tech environment to rely on such an analog relic.

A knock at the door interrupted Josh's concentration as he said, "Come in." Peter Hamilton had done hundreds of interviews for the *Wall Street Journal*; as he walked in, he thought, OK, here we go again.

Peter, over six feet tall and around forty-five years old, had a ruddy complexion but piercing blue eyes. He was recognized in the business world as a tough yet fair reporter. Josh had agreed to the interview simply because he had been impressed by Peter's proper treatment of other CEOs, even if there were obvious complex issues. He felt like he was hard but fair.

Josh relaxed as he rose and asked Peter to come in. Peter seemed somewhat surprised at Josh's height, almost six feet seven inches, and his youthful, athletic appearance. It wasn't often someone towered over him. Peter was intimidated, rarely running into anyone who towered over him like Josh. Even though he had read that Josh was tall, he still wasn't prepared to face him in such a small space. Regardless, he got over it quickly and felt confident in his preparation since he had worked hard preparing for this interview.

"Good morning, Peter; my name is Josh Douglas."

"It is a pleasure to meet you, Josh. I have been looking forward to our conversation."

"I have, as well, Peter. Do you mind if we go by first names?"

"Not at all, Josh; I prefer it. I appreciate you making time to have this interview. I know you must have a lot going on."

"I do, Peter, but I'm looking forward to this moment. Please have a seat; I hope this small room will be sufficient."

"It will be fine, Josh. Shall we begin?"

As Peter sat, he thought to himself, such a comfortable person to be around. Nevertheless, I must keep in mind my purpose here—to unearth the reasons behind Generation One's success. Peter was determined to discover who or what it was; both would be terrific stories.

2

An Unexpected Concept

"Thank you, Josh. I'm from the *Wall Street Journal*. Your impact has certainly made waves, and I'm excited to get to know each other and explore the intricacies of Generation One," the journalist expressed.

"Thanks, Peter. Good to have you here," Josh chuckled.

The two exchanged smiles.

"I've read many of your articles, Peter, and I appreciate your candid style. This is a perfect moment for a chat before the presentation. Let's make the most of this calm before the storm," Josh suggested.

"I've got many questions about your company, Generation One, but I also aim to glean some insights or thoughts about your success. Your openness to discuss your company and journey is appreciated; I also hope you'll allow me to delve deeper into your life. My readers are keen to learn more about you. Your influence in the business realm is significant. Many of our readers are eager to gain a deeper understanding of you, or at least more than what they currently know. I'm hoping you could shed some light on how you've navigated Generation One to its current market dominance. I, for one, have been anticipating learning some of your secrets. Would you mind if I use a tape recorder to ensure accuracy in capturing our conversation?"

"Sure thing," Josh agreed to record their conversation.

"Apologies for not having refreshments right now, but we can arrange something later if you prefer. There's a coffee shop across the street at the University Center."

"No issue, I'm fine, Josh," Peter responded, despite thinking that the chairs were a tad small for both, yet they were comfortable.

"How can I assist you?" Josh inquired, acknowledging the value of Peter's time.

"Well, allow me to start by expressing my gratitude for the time you're dedicating to this; I appreciate you carving out time from what must be a frantic day for you. I was apprehensive about your availability, considering the announcement you'll make in a few hours," Peter began.

"Not at all, Peter; I'm pleased we can utilize these moments to familiarize ourselves with each other and address any queries you have. Frankly, there's nothing else I'd rather do," Josh replied, his gaze fixed on Peter as he placed a small digital recorder between them on the antique table between the two chairs. The table had a small lamp, the room's only light source.

"Josh, you founded Generation One about a decade ago; is that accurate?" Peter asked.

"Yes, Peter, it was approximately ten years ago when a group of friends and I launched the company. However, in truth, the concept began brewing in my mind about three years prior. The original idea struck me as I was completing my MBA at the University of Texas Graduate School of Business. After completing my program, I joined a competitor to absorb as much knowledge as possible about the industry. I learned a great deal and owed them immensely for introducing me to this captivating industry and its advancements to our world," Josh explained.

"How long did you work there?" Peter asked.

"I was there for about four years. During that time, I delved deep into understanding the industry and honing my management skills. It was a period of constant reflection on how I'd run my own business in the future," Josh reflected.

"After those four years, how did you achieve such an impressive start? You seemed to hit the ground running; can you explain how your company managed such a swift takeoff?"

Peter inquired, adjusting the small recording device on the table.

Josh paused as if searching for the right words. "Well, it might seem that way, but our progress, particularly in the initial years, was slow and steady. I was fortunate to identify some exceptional colleagues who, in almost all cases, had significantly more industry experience than I did.

They were patient with my youth and guided me in countless ways. They bought into our ideas and believed in a superior way to establish a company. They played a crucial role in shaping our initial thinking and were instrumental in our company making some pivotal decisions early on. My sole objective was not to hinder their progress and to help overcome any early obstacles we encountered. We've always operated as a true team. I hope I provided energy and a youthful vision of our possibilities. I credit them for elevating those ideas to an entirely new level."

"You achieved success early on; you must have had a compelling vision for the business operations and the company's future."

"Yes, I had a clear direction for us, but my initial vision has evolved significantly over the past decade, thanks to invaluable insights from others and the continuous learning all our team members are encouraged to do. We worked persistently towards our goal of building a 'better' company that would make a significant contribution. We've always valued our people and their time, energy, and efforts. It's our people that have propelled us forward. We, as a team, are extremely proud of our progress and feel like we're moving in the right direction," Josh said, jotting down a quick note on his open portfolio as he conversed with Peter.

Peter studied the young man intently, reflecting on his maturity and tranquility. He found Josh's intensity, easygoing nature, and humility charming and honestly a bit disarming. It seemed so unlikely to encounter someone so young thriving in the cutthroat world of Big Business. He also looked at the well-worn folio, with pages containing countless jottings and ideas. So many things had been written on these well-used pages. There must be a story there, Peter mused.

"How can you account, other than utilizing this great team you assembled, for Generation One's phenomenal success? Is there a key you could share? Did you have some guiding principle that led you to make strategic moves? Was it from your program in Texas or your experience at your previous employer? Was someone in your life the catalyst for providing this clarity for the company's future?" Peter asked, turning slightly in his seat to face Josh more directly.

"Well, there are numerous factors I could point to. The insights from my colleagues, my faculty both in college and in Texas, and my family have been instrumental in shaping my worldview and our business. Moreover, I conducted extensive research and due diligence before moving forward. However, my primary guiding principle was consistently utilizing the 'magic of a moment.' I credit Mr. Mac, a long-time friend, for the results and focus I have today. His influence on me early in my life was profound. His principles and guidance have had an extraordinary impact on me and Generation One," Josh revealed.

"Josh, I'm intrigued. You mentioned the 'magic of a moment.' What does that mean? Who's Mr. Mac? Is it a personal philosophy you've applied to your work?" Peter inquired, curious.

Josh reclined in his chair and paused for a moment. A relaxed smile spread across his face as he looked directly at Peter and said, "Oh yes, Peter, it's a guiding focus for me, and yes, it's something I incorporated long ago that has been instrumental in how I tackle life's challenges as well as those in my professional life. Mr. Mac's assistance in cementing this practice in my life was pivotal in my personal development and, of course, how I approach my work at Generation One. Of all the things I've learned, the magic of a moment is the most important and significant guiding principle in my life."

"Could you elaborate on it? I'm curious to learn more about it and how it has guided your work and leadership at the company."

"Peter, I'd be delighted to share it with you. I'll need to explain the process I underwent to learn this concept. I've only shared it with a select few friends, but if you think it might be of interest to your readers, I'm happy to explain the concept and the process I underwent to learn it. It will be my pleasure. However, you have to make one promise."

"What would that be?"

"If you think we're veering off or if it's not engaging, just say, 'I think I've heard enough about this magic of a moment and Mr. Mac.' I'd be glad to focus on your other questions. Ask away," Josh offered.

"Josh, that sounds excellent; I'm hoping it will provide our readers with a deeper understanding of you, your style, and, of course, the success of Generation One," Peter responded.

"OK, Peter, I'm confident you'll find plenty that will be useful. Allow me to start with how I remember it; please make yourself comfortable," Josh concluded.

3

Introducing Mr. Mac

"Peter, I'll share my story from where it all began. It was ages ago, but those weeks were pivotal. So, you can imagine, it's quite vivid in my memory.

"Now, twenty years ago, it was scorching that day, the kind of sticky heat unique to the South. Unusual for Daytona Beach, Florida, there was no breeze; I was a sweaty mess. Typically, the sea breeze swept through, but that day, on the mainland where I lived, there was none. It was a little strange that day, with no breeze, totally still. The humidity was so thick and sweat dripped down the back of my shirt and off the end of my nose. More information than you want or need to know. It re-defined hot, and I wished my mom would let me go to the pool down at the YMCA, but she wouldn't. She wanted me to stay around the neighborhood. To say I wasn't happy about her decision is an understatement, but I accepted her less-than-agreeable verdict. But I sure thought it was an excellent reason to mope and stagger down the street. You know, kid stuff, totally miserable, wandering down the road. As I think about it now, what else would you expect during the first week of June in Daytona? Summer was upon us, even though most of it was still to come.

"I had lived there on Imperial Drive for almost five years. Feeling a sense of ownership, our street resembled many others on the Daytona Mainland—nondescript houses lining up in succession. Yeah, the Mainland, not the sea breeze side, where they always benefited from the constant breeze off the ocean.

"Our street was just one cinder block home after another, some with additions, mostly garages that had been reclaimed as additional rooms for the families that seemed to be in a never-ending growth mode. Everyone on the street knew each other. Most families have lived here since the neighborhood was built almost ten years ago. It's a funny thing, Peter, pretty strange. I think about it now; no one, or rarely, left Imperial Drive. At least, that is how I remember it. As a lower-middle-class neighborhood, how socially mobile could people be?

"I was the oldest of a family of three boys. My dad and mom split up when I was five, and my two younger brothers, Steve and Earl, and I lived on this street for our entire life. It was a comfortable place to live if it was our home for no other reason. As you can imagine, three boys got into much mischief but mostly played outside all day and had fun.

"My brothers and our friends had explored every inch of the woods and the streets in the neighborhood. Bike races up and down the streets and following the mosquito spraying trucks. As I think about it now, it wasn't the smartest thing in the world to do."

Peter laughed out loud at that. "Well, Josh, as kids, we all do stupid things, don't we? It's a miracle we all survive."

"Yes, so true, Peter," Josh joined in the laugh.

"There always seemed to be a pick-up baseball game or a race on our bikes down the streets. Plus, we would bike up and down the main roads looking for Coke bottles to take them to the store to collect our rewards and buy candy or something cold to drink.

"There was nothing we missed and nothing we didn't feel comfortable getting into, regardless of the future consequences. It was the type of neighborhood where you ate as many meals on your bike or at one of your friends' homes as you did at your own. When you did eat at home, it was usually with a bunch of your buddies or even with Colleen, who lived across the road. Colleen was our age, but after all, she was a girl. Funny now, she is the only girl I can remember on the street!

"Like so many others, the neighborhood was built in the mid-fifties to accommodate the incredible number of people moving into Central Florida, specifically into the Daytona area. Many 'race fans' couldn't stand to be farther than a few miles from the Daytona Speedway or young adults who fondly remembered Easter Break on the beach.

"A typical day, especially during the summer, was running out of the house not fifteen minutes after getting up, eating some Cheerios, and seeing what we could explore or do in the daylight hours. Most days were spent in pick-up football and baseball games, racing our bikes, or various forms of hide-and-seek. In hindsight, we always found ourselves occupied, never lacking activities.

"Mom usually didn't see us until dark, only after she started screaming at the top of her lungs, 'Boys, time to come home for dinner!' The incredible thing was that no matter where we were in the neighborhood or what we were doing, we could always hear her and come running for something to eat.

"We often ran into the house and told her one fantastic tale after another of our great exploits during the day. Heck, some of them were even true.

"This day, I dragged myself home, trying my best to stay calm. Failing, by the way. Walking down the road, I was about halfway down the street when I passed old 'Mr. Mac's house.' 'Mr. Mac,' as we all called him, had lived in the same house at 4107 Imperial Dr. for ten years. Strange, but I can still remember his home, its color, and the number on the side of his garage. His garage wasn't closed in and was rarely closed. As I said earlier, most people in those days converted their one-stall garages into another room, usually another bedroom, for their ever-growing families.

"Mr. Mac was among the first to move into the neighborhood around 1956. Mr. Mac looked old, and he probably was only about sixty, but for all I knew, as a young teenage boy, anyone over forty seemed like they were ancient. Mr. Mac was only fifty-six.

"Mr. Mac was one of the friendliest old guys on our street. His wife had died about three years earlier in a car accident. Everyone on the road was sad for Mr. Mac. We all thought he might leave the neighborhood after her death, but he didn't. We knew they were very close because you could see them on the front porch almost every night, talking and sharing a glass of tea. They liked each other and enjoyed each other's company. Still, I wouldn't say I like the thought of the loss he experienced, even to this day.

"As I think back to this day, which is burnt into my consciousness, I remember looking up and seeing Mr. Mac on his porch. Like so many other days, he was absorbed in his work. You could always see Mr. Mac working on something or involved in some activity when you went by his house. It didn't matter what time of day it was; it could be 5 a.m. or 10 p.m., and not that mom would ever let us out of the house that late at night. You could always find him puttering around his house, garage, or yard, always working on something.

"One of Mr. Mac's most incredible things was fixing old cars in his garage. His garage door was often left open, inviting us neighborhood boys to watch him tinker with those old cars. He always had time for us, embracing our relentless curiosity and admiration for his skill in dismantling and reassembling entire cars. Most old vehicles came to the garage with a tow from Mr. Mac's red Chevy pickup truck. He would move the old car into his garage, usually having to push it to its final parked location.

"He would then start the process of disassembling the entire vehicle. By completing it, he was down to the frame, wheels, and everything else on the benches surrounding the garage. Then, slowly, methodically, he would begin to put all the pieces back together. Some he would have to replace, some he would have to refurbish, but it was almost magic watching it all come together again. Often, he would work on a single piece all day and night to bring it back to mint condition. Amazingly, the whole thing would begin to shape in pristine shape. Even as a young boy, I thought what a miracle it was.

"Just the week before, I remember he had been working on an old black model T that must have been built around the turn of the century. It was in terrible condition when he had it towed into the garage. He carefully worked on the engine, such as it was, and put it back in the car. It always amazed me he could even find parts for these old relics, but he did. My brothers, I, and the Evans boys occasionally ventured into his garage. We would spend most of the afternoon watching him work and fetching various tools at his request. Of course, his payment for these services was our endless stream of questions and thoughts about the old car. You know, 'How old is it? Will it run again? I wonder who owned it before. Will you sell it? How much is it worth?' That was typical for a bunch of young teenage boys. He never seemed to tire of anything we said and always seemed to have time to listen to us, and he did.

"In addition to his cars, you could also see him working on his sailboat, which he dearly loved and kept in the backyard under a covered pad he built about five years ago, not long before his wife died. His wife loved to sail, and they would often go off for a week or two sailing, right up to the time she went to the store for some milk and never came back.

"After her death, he kept the boat under cover most of the time, except for about every week or so when he would remove the lid and carefully clean it from top to bottom. Almost a year ago, he began to take it out on his own, but you could tell it wasn't the same as when his wife was alive, and they would go together. We refrained from discussing the boat or his late wife, but he clearly missed her deeply.

"Peter, I know this is not a hard-hitting account of my business processes. Would you like me to continue?"

"Josh, I would love for you to continue," Peter responded. "I am fascinated by your recounting and am eager to understand how this older man made such a lasting impression on you. It's interesting that you still refer to him as Mr. Mac."

"He will forever be Mr. Mac to me," replied Josh fondly. "He is one of the most important people in my life; I aspire to be half the person he is. I guess calling him Mr. Mac is my way of expressing my respect for him. Let me continue then."

4

The Lessons Begin

"Thanks, Peter. Let me continue. One day, I saw Mr. Mac reading a book that seemed a foot thick. As a young kid, any book larger than your hand might as well have been an encyclopedia."

Josh waved at Mr. Mac and said, "How are you doing today, Mr. Mac?"

"Doing alright, Josh. How about you?" Mac replied, placing a bookmark in his book. His full head of gray hair and brilliant blue eyes often twinkled as he spoke. He always seemed welcoming and never appeared upset by interruptions, even from young boys like me.

Josh explained that he just returned from playing ball and wanted to go to the pool, but his mom told him to stay around the neighborhood. He decided to visit Mr. Mac, so he walked over to the front porch and sat in the rocking chair usually occupied by Mr. Mac's wife.

The porch was beautiful, with a wide assortment of flowers and several books neatly stacked on a table between two chairs. A worn folio was always close to Mr. Mac, who constantly wrote notes.

Josh looked at the thick book and expressed his doubts about being able to read something so significant. Mr. Mac assured him that he could read it and many other books if he learned the magic of a moment.

Curious, Josh asked what he meant by that. If he had a few minutes, Mr. Mac offered to tell him about it. Josh agreed, eager to learn anything that could help him read faster.

Mr. Mac explained that the magic of a moment was a concept that could be applied to many aspects of life, not just reading. He told Josh that understanding and consistently using this concept could make a real difference in his life.

Josh admitted he needed to improve at reading and was discouraged when faced with large books. Mr. Mac reassured him that the magic of a moment was not about reading quickly but learning and experiencing the concept.

Mr. Mac asked if Josh was ready to commit to learning about the magic of a moment. He explained that it would require effort and application in all aspects of his life. Josh agreed, excited about the prospect of improving his reading skills.

They decided to begin their discussions the following week, and over the next six to seven weeks, Mr. Mac taught Josh about the magic of a moment. This simple conversation with an older man on Imperial Drive set Josh on a new life path that he has followed for almost twenty years.

Peter asked if Josh still kept in touch with Mr. Mac, and Josh confirmed that they remained close friends, even after he moved away from Imperial Drive. He expressed his gratitude for Mr. Mac's wisdom and promised to reveal the magic of a moment to Peter and their readers.

Yes, Mr. Mac is still alive; he is almost eighty and lives independently in a condo in Florida. Josh stays in touch with him and always will for the remainder of Mr. Mac's life. Interestingly, even though Josh moved on, moved away, and left Imperial Drive after attending college, Mr. Mac remains one of his closest friends and confidants. Josh genuinely values every moment they have shared and believes Peter would like him.

"I'm sure I would," Peter said. "So, what did he tell you about the magic of a moment? I really want to know, and I'm guessing our readers will too."

"No problem," Josh replied. "It's my pleasure to continue telling you about the story that literally changed my life, and the wisdom Mr. Mac imparted to me."

5

Embrace the Potential of a Moment

They rocked in their respective chairs and waved as Mrs. Ford and Colleen drove down the road. Colleen's home was opposite Josh's on the street. Colleen always had her mom pick her up at school; she hated walking from school, especially if it was hot like today, so it was no different on a hot summer day.

Mr. Mac sat straight and tall in his chair, leaned slightly on the table beside him, and spoke quietly to Josh. "Let me ask you a question. What do you usually do on these Tuesday afternoons when you come home from school? Do you mind telling me?"

Josh looked at Mr. Mac and said, "Not much, to be honest; usually, I just run around the neighborhood with my brothers and our friends. We ride our bikes, collect Coke bottles, and take them to get some money or watch TV. See, there is nothing that special about what I do. In fact, until you asked, I typically couldn't have told you what I do. It's sort of like the day just happens and then seems to disappear for me."

Mr. Mac sat back in his chair, looked out on the street, and then slowly looked over at Josh and said, "OK, for the next weeks, starting today, why don't we meet for a couple of minutes on Tuesday afternoons, about this time? Since you don't usually have much going on except killing time, we will find a way to use some of these moments a bit more constructively. Does that sound alright with you?"

"That would be great. I would like that, especially if I could learn the magic of a moment." Josh paused momentarily and thought, I hope this is a good use of time. I would hate to waste time. I better ask him. I don't want to be doing something dorky.

"Mr. Mac, is this magic of a moment really special?" Josh quickly added, "I don't want to waste *your* time if it isn't."

"Josh, tell me honestly, why are you asking me that?"

"Well, I don't know. I mean, I know you have a lot you like to do around the house, including working on your cars. Plus, you know, I would hate to do something that was stupid, no offense to you, Mr. Mac. But if it will help me read books better and do more stuff, it might help me as I'm getting ready for college. You know that is just around the corner for me."

"No, no, Josh, no offense taken. I'll tell you what, if at any time you feel like this is stupid or a waste of your time, you can stop. I would never want you to do something you thought was a stupid waste of time. No problem, and we will still be friends, OK?"

"That would be great, Mr. Mac, thanks."

"One thing I need to know, Josh. I need to know that you really want to do this and will commit to do what you say you will do. I need you to promise me, and if you do, I promise to teach you. In no way is this a waste of my time. In addition, I promise nothing I ask you to do will be that hard. Sometimes you may wonder what I'm trying to teach you, but I promise you, it will become crystal clear. Trust me, everything will help you get in touch with the truth and power behind the magic of a moment."

With this, Mr. Mac looked at Josh with an easy smile but serious intention in his eyes.

"You got it, Mr. Mac; I promise to give it my best."

"I'll tell you what, don't worry about "your best," and say you'll do it, OK?"

"I will!"

"Great, can't ask for more than your best. By the way, you didn't know it, but you just gave a perfect magic of a moment response. Remember Josh, we can only say yes or no to life. There isn't any maybe; it's yes or no. Let that be your bond and your first lesson. Be decisive and answer the call of life with either a yes or a no. Make your goal to never be wishy-washy in how you face and deal with life. It is way too valuable to live that way. It's way too valuable!"

"Mr. Mac, this seems essential to you. I don't understand, but I'm willing to give my best; I will do it."

"OK, we will meet every Tuesday, but I will need to have you do some, well, homework before each meeting. It will mean that you must do something every day, OK?"

As a teenage boy, Josh thought homework was just what he needed: more reading. He thought about this for a minute and then said to Mr. Mac, "OK, as long as it doesn't take too long because I don't have much time, you know?"

"OK, we'll see if you have time or not. Let's start next Tuesday at this time and see how the first week of homework goes. Does that seem fair?"

"You got it. I better get going; I need to get home. So we will start next Tuesday afternoon, right?"

"Not quite so fast. I'm going to keep you just a moment longer if you have a moment more. Before you leave, don't you want to hear your homework? Tell you what, we will call it your assignment. Is that better?"

"Yes, Mr. Mac, an assignment sounds better." Josh smiled at him.

Mr. Mac said, "I know you can't wait to hear how tough this will be, can you?" Mac smiled to himself as he looked intently at Josh.

"Well, I was wondering if you were going to tell me, Mr. Mac, or if we were just going to start next week. OK, let me have it. What is my first assignment for the week, or will you let me off the hook this first week? I know better; I figure you aren't going to let me off that easy, are you?"

Mr. Mac leaned forward in his chair and said, "No, Josh, I'm not going to let you off that easy. You seem to be ready to tackle this process, and I sure don't want to let you down! I really like your enthusiasm and willingness to jump right into this, even if you aren't completely clear what you're jumping into. It makes me glad we are going to take this little journey together."

"Yes, I really want to learn about this concept of the magic of a moment, especially if it will help me at school or at home. I feel like I'm starting to fall behind, so if I can accomplish half as much as you do, I will be thrilled. I mean it; I'll feel like a million dollars."

"You have no idea how close to the truth what you just said is Josh, no idea! OK, let's start. Let me ask you a question, Josh—do you have to do any chores at home? You know, something your mom wants you to do, especially if you have to do it on a regular basis?"

"Oh yeah, I sure do. She is always asking me to do things; I think because I'm the oldest. I mean, I don't mind helping, but I tell you what, it's not like I have all the time in the world." Josh looked at Mac and wondered if he knew how busy he was. He got up because he was feeling uncomfortable for some reason.

"I know you have a lot to do or at least a lot of things you want to do, like run around with your friends. Doing things with your friends is an important part of your life right now. So, what are some of the things your mother asks you to do, if you don't mind me asking?"

"Sometimes, I must wash dishes, mow the yard, and take out the garbage daily. I don't mind taking my time to cut the yard; it helps my mom out, and she needs the help; after all, I'm the oldest, so it's only fitting for me to do it.

Mr. Mac looked at Josh for a minute and didn't say a thing, like he was waiting for him to say something else. "Which one of those three chores do you really dislike doing the most? You know, the thing you just can't stand and end up never finding any time to do it?"

"Well, I only wash dishes every so often, so I can deal with that; you know, sort of taking my turn, which is the right thing to do. Like I said, I don't mind mowing the yard because it has always made me feel like, well, more like a grown-up, but taking the garbage out is such a pain, you know what I mean?"

"No, I'm not sure I understand, but let's talk about it a minute more. You hate to take out the garbage because it takes so much time, or do you hate it because you feel like it's always needing to be done?"

"No, not that; in fact, it usually only takes me a minute or two, that's not it. In fact, it's not that at all, but I usually must get up because mom tells me to take it out. It never occurs at a convenient time."

Josh felt a little weird. "What if there was a way for you never to have to worry about it again? Mr. Mac inquired. "Would you be interested in hearing about it?"

"Yes, I would like to hear what you have to say, but if it doesn't, you aren't going to change my mind about it. I will always hate it, and it will always be a pain." Josh started pacing in front of Mr. Mac and went on, "You know, this is the type of thing we have to do when growing up that is just what we have to deal with, as much as a pain as it might be. I would love to make it a non-issue, but I don't see how that can happen."

"Well, it can. In fact, it will just take a moment of your time, a magical moment, in fact."

"You need to know that I'm pretty skeptical, but I still want you to know it."

"Sure, remember we are talking about the magic of a moment, right? I'm going to do more than tell you; I'm going to show you how it can happen."

"With garbage," Josh laughed out loud.

"OK, if you say so, great," Josh added. "I still don't understand how something like taking out the garbage has anything to do with the Magic of a Moment, but give it a shot and tell me or, as you said, show me."

"Well, Josh, here is the key, the key you are going to learn this week. You won't even have to write this down. I just want you to listen and do exactly what I tell you to do. OK? At this point in the process, it is much more important to do what I say and then question and process it after you have done it and experienced the power of the magic of a moment. OK?"

"OK, sure, I will do it. If you can tell me a way not to think about it anymore, I'm all ears."

"Well, I promise you, you will be amazed at what is going to happen if you just do exactly what I say."

"OK, what do I need to do?"

"OK, now remember, you will do just as I tell you. For the next week, I want you to act immediately as soon as you think about taking out the garbage. In other words, the minute you think about 'having' to take out the garbage, I want you to jump up and do it. No hesitation, no delay; do it immediately. OK?"

"That is my homework, to jump up and take out the garbage immediately and not think about it, just do it. You mean you just want me to do it right away?"

"Yes, that's what I'm asking you to do for this next week. Oh yeah, and one other thing as you are taking it out. I want you to be conscious of how much time it takes you and how, if in any way, it changes your feeling about this chore. That's it; that is your assignment for this next week. See, I told you it wasn't going to be that bad. Is it?"

"No, Mr. Mac, I can handle that; we'll see what happens. I'll let you know when we meet next week. Does 3 p.m. sound OK with you?"

"Sure, Josh, I'll see you here then. Have a great week; I will look forward to our time together next week. Have a great one."

"OK, I'll do it, but what about the magic of a moment? How am I going to learn about it? What do I need to do to know about it?"

"I'll tell you what, Josh, for the next week, all I'm going to ask of you is to remember this one task, and we'll talk about it when you come back next week. Is that OK with you?"

"Yes, it's fine, but I thought I would need to do something else, something special, to learn about the magic of a moment."

"You do, but that will come along as we go through the weeks. Starting today, when you get home, this will be all you have to do for this week. So, do we have a deal?"

"You bet; it seems easy, but you have a deal."

6

Act Now

"Well, Peter, I hope I haven't bored you too much," said Josh.

"Not at all, Josh. I'm enjoying hearing about the magic of a moment and especially how important Mr. Mac was in your life. If it's okay with you, I would like to know the rest of the story. You know, for both of you. His willingness to give his time and your willingness to listen as a young teenager is impressive. I admire the practical way he was talking with you. He really took time with you. Please continue."

Josh continued, "I can tell you that on that first day, I wondered if this was some waste of time. But as I walked home, I started to feel more and more like this was an easy thing to do. I'm unsure what to learn, but I'm willing to try it. Plus, Mr. Mac was so sincere about helping me. Why not give it a try and see what happens? After all, he was right. It would only take me a moment to take the garbage out. I'm not sure why I didn't think of that, but I didn't. Heck, it might even make it easier for me."

Peter asked, "So what about the garbage? Did you do it? By the way, Josh, that may be the strangest question I've ever asked anyone."

Laughing, Josh replied, "Peter, let me tell you, you know what the first thing I did when I got home? I went straight to the kitchen and took out the garbage. When my mom got home from work and found that I had taken it out, she couldn't believe it. Smiling, I was a bit proud of myself, too."

Josh's mom had said, "Josh, did you take out the garbage? I didn't even have to ask you. Bravo!"

"Peter, it made me feel so good. She was happy, and it was such a small thing. It felt good that she didn't have to bug me or anything. I don't know, it made me feel powerful in a way and like a load was taken off my shoulder. Plus, it wasn't going through my mind repeatedly. Does that make sense? I mean, it was such a small thing, just taking out the garbage."

Peter replied, "You know, Josh, I can relate to that for sure. I know there are things I put off in my life all of the time. Instead of just doing them, I keep putting them off. Most of the time, I spend much more of my time thinking or worrying about something rather than just doing it. The time to do it is often a fraction of the time I spend thinking about it and putting it off."

Josh agreed, "So true, Peter. It was true for me. Honestly, I did it for the rest of the week. As soon as I thought about it, I took action and did it. No fuss, no muss. Just do it. I hardly thought about it. In fact, the strange thing is that I thought about it less than I had before, a lot less. It came to my mind, and I just did it, and then I was clear to think about other things. So simple but so profound."

Josh continued, "Let me continue…as promised, one week later, I came back for my meeting with Mr. Mac, surprised at what had occurred. Still, for some reason, I think about him and the magic of a moment concept often, especially when I'm tempted to put something off. Every time I took out the garbage, but more than that. I was figuring out how immediately acting on something as small as taking out the trash could make me feel so good. I was totally surprised. I looked forward to telling Mr. Mac, and I can also tell you how I was very interested to find out about the next 'home-work' assignment."

Josh had trotted over to Mr. Mac's house, arriving early. He wanted to talk with him about what he had experienced.

"Hi, Josh," Mr. Mac greeted him as he jogged to his porch. He looked like he was working on some outline, but he laid it down when Josh came up and flopped in his chair.

"HI there, Mr. Mac. How are things going with you? What are you doing? Looks like you sure are making a lot of notes. Of course, that's no surprise."

"Oh, this, Josh? I keep notes of things I need or want to do. I'm always writing little messages to myself about everything I want to do, so they are off my mind but also retrievable. It's a way to communicate with my future self. It is always helpful to get them on paper before I forget them. On top of that, I don't have to worry about them anymore.

"So, how did you do with your homework assignment? How did the garbage taking out go—your first lesson?"

Josh agreed to tell Mr. Mac about his experience but had a question first. "Sure, go ahead, Josh," said Mr. Mac.

Josh asked, "About what you just said, do you always write down what you need or want to do? Doesn't that take a lot of time? Doesn't that mean you are always carrying a notebook around with you? Also, what do you mean by 'future me'?"

Mr. Mac answered Josh's questions and explained how having a journal with him all the time had served him well. He suggested that they discuss how Josh might use this idea as his next homework assignment after discussing his experience from the past week.

"Oh yes, the 'future me,'" Mr. Mac repeated. "Josh, that is me when I get around to something that might not remember what the current me wanted to do."

"That makes sense to me, Mr. Mac. I often forget the ideas I get."

Josh then began sharing his experience with Mr. Mac. Mac explained the concept of procrastination and how it could make tasks seem more significant than they were.

Josh understood the concept but wondered how it would apply to more extensive projects or tasks requiring more time and effort than simply taking out the garbage.

Mr. Mac acknowledged the question as a good point and explained how breaking tasks into smaller steps and taking consistent action could make even larger projects more manageable. He emphasized the importance of knowing what one wants and promised to discuss this further in future lessons. As they continued their conversation, Josh understood more about the magic of a moment and how it could be applied to various aspects of his life.

"Well, Josh, why don't you tell me exactly what you learned?" Mr. Mac asked.

Josh thought momentarily, then said, "Act immediately, and don't put off a task when you think about it. There is real power in acting on what you need to do, and the opposite is also true."

"What do you mean, Josh?" Mr. Mac inquired.

"What I mean is that if you don't act on what you need to do, you begin to actually lose momentum and energy. It's like it saps you of energy. Does that make sense?"

"Yes, Josh, that is really very perceptive of you. That is excellent, Josh; I mean it. That is exactly what I wanted you to learn.

"Okay, I'm convinced you learned a lot. By the way, I know this next lesson won't be as easy as taking out the garbage can, but it actually will be if you break it down to something that seems a little bit more manageable. You see, Josh, everything in life has a series of small tasks. It's like reading a book; yes, you are reading an entire book, but in actuality, you are reading a chapter at a time, a paragraph at a time, a sentence at a time, even a word at a time. So it is with almost everything if we can just break it down into smaller, more manageable activities, many of which just take a moment to do. Plus, when you do that, something amazing happens that I don't want to tell you about until you experience it yourself. So for this next week, what I want you to do is every time you think about needing to read your book, I want you to pick it up and read at least one page. If after you read that one page, or the moment it will take to do it, if you want to stop, stop. However, if you want to and it's convenient to do it, keep reading another page. Then just let whatever happens happen. Does that seem reasonable?"

"Sure, I can do that, no problem. Let me make sure I understand. If I think about reading the book, I pick it up and read a page. If I don't feel like continuing, I put it down until I feel like reading it again. Is that it?"

"Yes. You got it. I do want to make one more request of you, though, and this might be a little tough. I want you to keep the book with you as often as possible. Just in case you think about it and have a free moment to read it. I know you may feel a little uncomfortable about that, but believe me, it will work. Are you willing to do that?"

"Well, my buddies are going to think I'm a little weird if I do it, but for this one week, I'll give it a try. It's a deal, Mr. Mac. I'm going to do it for this week. In fact, I'm going home right now and pick it up and read that first page."

"Okay, Josh, come back next week at the same time, and we'll talk about your progress. I'm glad you are taking immediate action to get your book. See, you're already learning the magic of a moment. I'll see you next week. Oh yes, will you still do the same thing you did last week with the garbage?"

"Sure, I will, Mr. Mac. It's like it doesn't exist anymore, you know, as a big deal, and I like that. In fact, I've been trying to do that with everything I have to do, and you know what? It works on almost everything, just like you said it would. I will see how it works with my reading, and we can talk about it next week. See you then. Have a great afternoon."

"See you then, Josh, have fun." Mac watched as Josh jumped up and ran down the street toward his house. He knew *Catcher in the Rye* was waiting for him. It was a good afternoon.

7

The Potential of Taking Action

"So, it seems like Mr. Mac made a difference in the way you approach your life and in such practical ways," Peter observed. "I like his simple messages and their applicability in many things. Josh, I've heard from interviews with your staff that you are someone who tackles things head-on and without delay. Did this simple exercise have that much impact on you?"

"Good question, Peter. The answer is yes, but it was just the beginning of how the magic of a moment changed my life," Josh replied. "Mr. Mac's teachings had a profound effect on me. I often return to the simplest teachings and concepts and call on them to decide and take action. This lesson was fundamental in understanding what I could do if I applied these concepts.

"In a nutshell, Mr. Mac taught me to tackle anything you want or need to do and always have a bias for action. In the simplest terms, I learned it's about acting immediately. It was a core concept, which you will clearly see as we go through each of the teachings. Most things in life give way or can be made better by taking action, no matter how small the type of action. The smallest of steps will eventually get you to your destination. I love the statement by Theodore Roosevelt in this regard; maybe you have heard it.

"Roosevelt said, 'It is not the critic who counts, not the man who points out how the strong man stumbled or where the doer of deeds could have done better, the credit belongs to the man who is actually in the arena; whose face is marred by dust and sweat and blood; who strives valiantly; who errs and comes short again and again...who knows the great enthusiasms, the great devotions, and spends himself in a worthy cause; who at the least knows, in the end, the triumph of high achievement; and who, at the worst, if he fails, at least fails while doing great, so that his place shall never be with those cold timid souls who know neither victory nor defeat.'

"I love this statement. It is all about wading into life and knowing you aren't always going to be successful, but if you don't try, you never know what is possible.

"So yes, this concept stuck with me. I act on things as soon as I think about them. I wouldn't say I like putting things off; I don't want to give them control over my life. I like to be more intentional about having the kind of life I want. The only way to do this is to take action. I realized in a very profound way if you don't do the things you can do, then you will never get to things you want to do."

Peter looked at Josh for a long time and said, "You mean it, don't you, Josh? So you use this in your personal life as well as your professional life? Something so profound must guide a lot you do. Again, I'm struck by how practical and straightforward it is. In almost all of life, there really is something you can always do."

"Sure, the concept works in all areas of life, from the most mundane to the most difficult of situations. It's just like the second lesson; it was one of the most powerful lessons of my life. Like the first simple lesson of taking action when you think about something as soon as you think about it and as soon as possible. In addition, the second concept of breaking down all tasks into a series of 'doable' activities has served me well. I will tell you about what I learned with the simple exercise of reading *Catcher in the Rye*. By the way, this is a lesson that I have used and deployed for my entire life since that summer when I was fourteen years old."

"Yeah, I heard that you are a voracious reader and that you always have a book nearby."

"Yes, that is true, but it's not just about reading books. It certainly works with that. It's about how to approach everything that enters your life. My experience is that everything has some next smaller, doable step. The key is to quickly identify that next step, decide to do something about it, or plan when you will. Let me share my experience with this concept, this second homework assignment."

"Great, I would love to hear it. Are we still OK with time?"

"Sure, Peter, we have plenty of time to talk. I'm just glad you are interested in hearing it."

"You know, Josh, I too often hear theories and concepts about business by leaders who only want to make an impression on my readers and their competitors. With you, I sense there is a comfort level within yourself and a realization that sometimes the most powerful things in life are simple yet meaningful. There is something so real, so simple about what you are saying, but at the same time powerful and illuminating to me." Peter gazed steadily at Josh with increasing admiration and many questions in his mind.

"Well, thank you, Peter, you are right; so often, my thoughts are simple and direct. I did learn that from Mr. Mac. I learned that the best approach is often the most direct approach. I feel comfortable with this approach and value taking things at face value and moving forward with whatever I find at hand. It has served me well both in my personal life and also in business."

"This is obvious, Josh. Tell me more about your second assignment if you would."

8

The Power of Immediate Action

In his youth, one might surmise that Josh was thrilled but doubtful about the task Mr. Mac had assigned him. He wrestled with reading and continually procrastinated, so eliminating it from his concerns was appealing, yet he confessed to some skepticism about its effectiveness.

Unexpectedly, he dashed home, grabbed his book, and began reading. Holding the book, he was torn between two thoughts. First, the book was considerably large, prompting him to consider seeking CliffsNotes

However, the second and more persuasive thought was his newfound belief in his ability to complete it. He was starting to trust Mr. Mac's advice. He truly did. He desired to test if Mr. Mac's words held any truth. After all, he had witnessed significant changes in mere days. The act of immediate action was beginning to transform his life in various ways. He found himself acting on minor tasks, which made him feel powerful and capable in a way he hadn't before. It was mostly for trivial things like picking up objects, taking out the trash, or running errands for his mother. Regardless of the task's nature, the ability to take immediate action made him feel like he was controlling his life. Oddly enough, it made him feel liberated and like he genuinely owned his life. So, what he was learning was working on bite-size issues, so now it was time to find out if it would work on something as big as reading a book.

"Josh," Peter observed, "I can see it was making a difference in you. Even as you talk about it now, I can see an enthusiasm about how you remember that time in your life.

"What is interesting to me is how, on your own, you saw how this could be applied to other things. I can see how it would make you feel more powerful and in control of your life; instead of *having* to do things, you were *choosing* to do them. That's a pretty major change, isn't it? But I guess the important question is, 'Did you finish the book?'"

"Great question, Peter," Josh responded enthusiastically, "I did, actually. I finished it by Sunday of that week."

The conversation continued with Josh sharing his experience and Peter expressing his curiosity about the outcomes. The dialogue revealed Mr. Mac's teachings' profound impact on Josh's life and how they transformed his attitude towards tasks and responsibilities.

As Josh approached Mr. Mac's porch for their next meeting, he noticed Mr. Mac working on his car in the garage. He greeted Josh and asked him to wait a few moments while he finished.

"No problem, Mr. Mac," Josh responded cheerfully, "I'm actually a little early."

Their conversation continued with Josh expressing his eagerness to learn more from Mr. Mac and Mr. Mac encouraging Josh's newfound interest in reading and proactive attitude towards life.

As Josh walked towards the porch after their conversation in the garage, he reflected on Mr. Mac's influence on his life and how much he desired to emulate Mr. Mac's efficiency and effectiveness.

"I appreciate your words, Peter," Josh replied. "I'm satisfied with my progress so far, but I'm aware that I have a lifetime of potential contributions ahead of me. I aspire to be half as productive as Mr. Mac in my life. We should get back to my story before time runs out. I want to respect your time and provide as much information as possible.

"Peter, let me go with my story and tell you what happened in my meeting with Mr. Mac."

As Josh settled into his usual spot on the porch, he absentmindedly opened his book, a habit he had formed over the past week. He had become so engrossed in the story that it felt like he was a part of it. Over the past week, he noticed a significant improvement in his concentration. He could easily immerse himself in any task or problem and feel at ease. The truth was, he yearned for more knowledge. He was eager to discover what lay on the next page and knew that whether it was a page, a chapter, or an entire book, he would progress if he started. "Even today, Peter, this remains true for me."

Let's return to your question, Josh thought. He saw Mr. Mac stepping out of the front door onto the porch. Mr. Mac had a large glass of lemonade and a chilled Coke for Josh.

"Here you go, Josh," said Mr. Mac, "I hope it's cold enough for you. I see you've done some reading—that's a good use of your time. It's funny, there's always time to do something if we take action, especially if it's something close at hand."

"You're right, Mr. Mac," Josh agreed, thanking him for the Coke. "When we started this two weeks ago, I wasn't sure if it would be worthwhile, but I've learned a lot since then.

"Two weeks ago, I would make a fuss over the simplest tasks, but now, I just do them. I feel silly for choosing to take out the garbage as my task, but now I realize I can apply this principle to many things. I make use of every moment of my day without feeling strained. I enjoy that. I feel like I'm growing as a person and improving my ability to get things done and achieve my goals."

As Mr. Mac settled into his chair, his gaze remained fixed on Josh. "The reality is, Josh," he began, "you're accomplishing things because you're taking action. It might sound like double talk, but it isn't. You're achieving more because you're doing more. You're learning to seize the moments and discovering the true value of this strategy. If you persist, you'll be amazed at what you can accomplish. You'll be able to do things that will astound you."

A broad smile spread across Josh's face. "You're right, Mr. Mac," he said. "I am achieving a lot more, and it's only been two weeks. I'm amazed at how such simple changes have made such a big difference in my life. Oh, and I wanted to tell you I finished *Catcher in the Rye* in four days. Can you believe that?"

"I'm very proud of you, Josh," said Mr. Mac. "Tell me about it."

"Mr. Mac, just as you suggested, I started carrying the book with me. Whenever I had a free moment or thought about it, I would read. As you probably expected, once I started reading, I would get interested in the story and keep reading. Often, I would read for over an hour. It was strange; suddenly, I couldn't get enough of the book. I was eager to know what would happen next, so I kept reading. What I loved most was that I never felt pressured; I was completely at ease. Actually, that's not entirely true—I started feeling anxious to return to the story. I began making time to read. Can you believe that? Josh Douglas looking forward to reading a book?"

"Good for you, Josh," said Mr. Mac. "I couldn't ask for a better application of the lesson. To be completely honest, I suspected this would happen. This is crucial to the 'magic of a moment' concept. It's about engaging with your life and not letting tasks pile up. It's about breaking any task down into manageable pieces. It's like the old riddle: 'How do you eat an elephant?' The answer is 'one bite at a time.' The only challenge in any task is knowing where to start and clearly knowing what to do first. Whether it's a book or a project, your first goal is to decide on the action and then to act. You discovered this with the book. In other complex life activities, it might be more complicated, but the principle of breaking down the task remains the same."

"So, Mr. Mac," Josh asked, "are you saying that I can apply this principle to everything in my life?"

"That's right, Josh," Mr. Mac confirmed. "I can assure you that this principle can be applied to everything in life—that's what makes it so exciting! Any task can be broken down into a couple or even several smaller tasks. Once you identify the task, as you did with your book, you simply start taking consistent action, and you'll accomplish a great deal. The problem most people face when starting a task they've been procrastinating on is that they simply don't know where to begin."

"The best part is that it really works," said Josh.

"Every time I thought about my reading, I would remember my promise to you and tell myself that I could do it, that I could read a page. The truth is, I never read just one page, not once. But I have a question: Why did I suddenly have time to read when I didn't before?"

"That's an important question, Josh," replied Mr. Mac.

"Let me give you two reasons. The first reason is simple: you read your book because you had it with you. We often don't do something because we don't have the necessary 'thing' close to us. You can't read a book you don't have. When you started carrying the book, you had it there to read whenever you thought about it. Moreover, having the book with you served as a reminder to read. It was a constant reminder that you could use the next few minutes to read at least a page, just like you did while waiting for me on the porch a few minutes ago. Most people simply forget or don't have the information they need to take action. This is true for a book or any project. Just having it with you was a reminder or trigger to act."

"What do you mean by 'trigger,' Mr. Mac?"

"What I mean is that our actions, thoughts, and even emotions often occur because they remind us of something we need to do or something we believe will happen. It's like seeing something sweet at home and craving it. It's a visual reminder of what you think will happen if you eat it. In this case, it's going to taste really good."

"That makes a lot of sense, Mr. Mac," said Josh. "I like the term 'trigger.' You're right—having the book with me made it easy for me to find time to work on it. No, more than that, it motivated me to keep working on it. It's funny how I had all these times during the day to make some progress, and I did. It felt good to do it and see progress towards my goal of reading the book. Plus, I started getting more interested in it. What was the second reason?"

"The second reason, the 'trigger,' has to do with a small part of our brain called the Reticular Activating System," Mr. Mac explained.

"What activating system?" Josh asked.

"Let me pause my story for a moment," said Josh to Peter. "Up until that point in my conversations with Mr. Mac, I thought he was just trying to give me some good advice, like a grandfather would. Then he mentioned this reticular activating system thing. I was fourteen and had no idea what he was talking about. But after his explanation, it's something that has stayed with me my entire life."

Peter looked at Josh and said, "So what did he say? I'm forty-seven years old, and I've never heard of that concept."

"It would be my pleasure to explain," said Josh. "Let me tell you what he told me."

Mr. Mac looked at Josh momentarily, then off into the distance. Then he turned back to Josh and said, "I'm trying to think of the best way to explain this so that it makes sense. Let me ask you a question: Is there something that you want right now in your life? Something that you don't have but would love to?"

"Of course, Mr. Mac," replied Josh. "There are many things, but there's one thing I really want: a truck to drive. I know I must wait a couple of years, but I want one so badly that I can taste it."

"I understand," said Mr. Mac. "I remember I wanted the same thing when I was your age. Is there a specific model or color you want?"

"Yes, I want a black Chevy half-ton," said Josh.

"Alright, good. You know what you want. Have you spotted many in the past week?" asked Mr. Mac.

"That's the strangest thing, Mr. Mac," Josh replied. "Now that you mention it, I see those trucks everywhere. Whether I'm biking to school or driving around town with my mom, they seem to be all over the place. What does this have to do with the reticular activating system?"

"Well, Josh," Mr. Mac began, "you're seeing them 'everywhere' because of the reticular activating system. This is why you managed to find time for your book. You had a goal—to read the book. You kept the book close to you or with you most of the time. Your reticular activating system reminded you that you could read a page or two. It allowed you to perceive the opportunities, just like it showed you all those black Chevy trucks while you were in town. Does that make sense?"

"I think I get it," Josh responded. "So, this part of my brain lets me focus on what I want?"

"Exactly," Mr. Mac confirmed. "That's what this part of your brain does. That's why having your work or reminders of your work nearby can help you achieve them more effectively."

"Is that why you always keep your portfolio so close, Mr. Mac?"

"Yes, Josh, it is," Mr. Mac replied. "I keep my ideas, tasks I want or need to do, along with strategies on how to accomplish them, in my portfolio. It's incredibly helpful. Simply having my portfolio with me allows me to jot down ideas, make a quick note on something I want to work on, or just brainstorm on paper. It's an excellent way to keep track of everything I want to do. And the best part is that it usually only takes a minute. You know, in a moment."

"Oh right, the 'magic of a moment.' Like taking out the trash or reading a book. You can use the same process, and it's really straightforward to do."

"Mr. Mac, I don't really need to worry about that," Josh interjected, "I don't have much to do. Honestly, most tasks I have are pretty simple; there's no need to write them down."

"Well, Josh," Mr. Mac countered, "I think you'd be surprised. I bet you have more tasks than you think or things you want to do. We'll make that your next assignment. Are you ready for it?"

"Sure, let's do it," Josh agreed.

"But before we move on," Mr. Mac added, "What did you learn from this assignment? I want to ensure you're comfortable with what you're learning."

"Well, Mr. Mac," Josh began, "I've learned to take immediate action and not procrastinate. I've learned to break down any task into smaller, manageable parts. I've also learned that my brain will prompt me into action through the reticular activating system if I have reminders of what I want to do readily available. And I've learned that no matter how daunting the task, there's always something I can do."

"That's an excellent summary of the first two lessons, Josh," Mr. Mac praised. "You're a fast learner and seem to be implementing these ideas well. Good job. So, are you ready to start the next lesson?"

"You bet, Mr. Mac, I'm ready!" Josh affirmed.

9

Seizing Life's Fleeting Moments

M r. Mac leaned back in his chair, taking a long sip from his condensation-covered lemonade, a necessary antidote to the ever-present heat in Daytona. He studied Josh briefly before asking, "Well, Josh, let me ask you this. Do you ever jot down what you want to do or thoughts that cross your mind throughout the day? You know, those spontaneous thoughts about your life, about what you might want to do someday or even right now?"

"No, Mr. Mac, I really don't. Like I said, there's not much to write down. Usually, I just sort of think about it and then move on to something else. I suppose, as you ask me this, I just store it in my mind, and usually something reminds me about it, or to be honest, I just lose it completely. I've noticed that you're always writing things down. I've wondered why you do that. To be honest, I thought it was because your memory wasn't very good. You know, because of your age. No offense, Mr. Mac."

"None taken, Josh," Mr. Mac replied. "The truth is, it's a habit I developed many years ago. I didn't learn the lessons I'm sharing with you until

I was much older than you are now. There were plenty of things in my life that seemed like good ideas at the moment I had them, but like you, I just lost them simply because I got distracted, busy, or simply forgot them. During every day, we all have thousands of thoughts. Like you, I would forget them or perhaps say in my mind, I'll get back to them at some point.

"One thing I know for sure, Josh, is that forgetting things isn't something that only happens with old people; it happens to all of us."

Josh paused, looking as if he was contemplating something. "You know, it's funny, Peter," he said. "I remember Mr. Mac laughing out loud but also seeming very intent on telling me more. Today, I realize how true it is. We all have insights and eureka moments, but for most of us, they are highly fleeting thoughts."

"I know what you mean, Josh," Peter agreed. "Because of my profession as a reporter, I tend to write a lot of observations down. We are trained to look and really see what is happening. Do you think that's what Mr. Mac was getting at? Was he also saying not just capture them but be intentional about noticing them?"

"I'm not sure, but he probably was. He often had multiple purposes when he was sharing these simple concepts. It was always true that I missed a lot, but by starting this exercise, I began to learn to see them. I know that sounds strange. The intention to write them down made me even more aware of how much I was missing. Let me continue and tell you what he said."

"That would be great, Josh," Peter responded eagerly.

"I'm interested in his perspective on this issue and how he used these moments to give you your next assignment."

"You already know him well. Let me go on."

Josh looked at Mr. Mac for a long moment, waited for his laughter to subside, and then said, "You didn't learn these things you're telling me until you were older? I thought you always were this way and had done what you are teaching me. I realize how crazy that is; I guess everyone has to learn the principles they use in their lives, don't they? We aren't born knowing how to use the moments of our lives."

"Indeed, we all have to learn," Mr. Mac told Josh. "I was around twenty-nine or thirty when my grandfather imparted these lessons to me during a series of discussions. He was a remarkable man with an infectious energy and style everyone admired and loved. His hero was Teddy Roosevelt, a man who, knowingly or not, practiced the magic of a moment throughout his life. Teddy was not just a president but a person who seized every moment of his life."

Josh interrupted Mr. Mac, asking, "Are you saying Teddy Roosevelt also practiced the magic of a moment?"

"Indeed, Josh," Mr. Mac replied. "He certainly applied many of the concepts. I could recount countless stories about Teddy, my hero, but suffice it to say he was always making the most of every moment. For instance, Teddy read two to three books a day during his presidency. Can you believe that?"

"No way, Mr. Mac," Josh responded in disbelief. "No one, not even a president, can do that. Especially not a president."

"But he did, Josh," Mr. Mac insisted. "He was an extraordinary man who was both gifted and disciplined in using the same magic of a moment concepts you're learning now. As we continue our discussions, you'll be fascinated by what we talk about and what you can apply in your life."

"Okay, Mr. Mac," Josh smiled and interrupted again. "I think it's cool that I'm learning something that Teddy Roosevelt used."

Mr. Mac returned with a smile. "You are indeed learning something valuable. Now, where was I? Ah, yes, I was a young husband and father who felt constantly rushed and as if I wasn't making meaningful progress with things that mattered to me. It was quite disheartening. My wife suggested we take a vacation to visit my grandfather in Cocoa Beach, Florida. Despite my initial reluctance due to financial concerns and work commitments, I eventually agreed."

Mr. Mac continued his story, detailing how they spent almost two weeks with his grandfather, fishing and spending time together. During this time, his grandfather shared the magic of a moment concept—the same concepts he was now sharing with Josh.

"Is your grandfather still alive?" Josh asked.

"No," Mr. Mac replied with a hint of melancholy. "He passed away at an old age, almost 100 years old. He remained vibrant and active until his final years. I miss him dearly."

"So, he taught you about the magic of a moment?"

"Yes, he did," Mr. Mac confirmed. "In fact, he gave me this old portfolio at the end of our vacation that I've used every day since then."

Josh noticed the worn portfolio on the bench beside Mr. Mac. "It looks like it's seen a lot of use," he remarked.

"It has indeed," Mr. Mac replied with a fond smile. "It's rarely far from my reach as it helps me capture my ideas, tasks, insights, and special comments."

"Are you going to ask me to do the same?" Josh asked, eyeing the portfolio.

"No, Josh," Mr. Mac responded, pulling out a small notepad with a pencil stuck in the rings. "For the next week, I want you to carry this pad and pencil with you at all times. Write down anything that comes to mind, whether it's something you need to do, want to do, or find interesting. You don't need to do anything with it; just keep it in your pocket and write down things as they come to you."

Josh agreed to the task, joking about how his friends would think he'd become a nerd if he started carrying around a portfolio like Mr. Mac. They shared a laugh before Josh stood up to leave.

"Same time next week, Mr. Mac?" Josh asked.

"Absolutely, Josh," Mr. Mac replied. "I'll see you then. Have a great week!"

"You too!" Josh called back as he walked away.

10

Capturing Inspiration

Peter excused himself to take a quick break and went down the hall. While Peter was gone, Josh took a moment to think back about his time with Mr. Mac. This entire interview made him reflect on how impactful Mr. Mac had been. Josh knew he was a particular person who would always impact his life.

This conversation and retelling of the story allowed him to remember how important Mr. Mac was and how much their relationship had changed his life. What he had accomplished, and the same direction he had taken, was influenced by these seven practices he incorporated into his life. A warm feeling filled his being, and he couldn't wait to continue the conversation with Peter.

Josh took out his now old, well-worn portfolio and opened it up to the first empty page. He wrote a note suggesting that he pull together all he had learned from Mr. Mac and consider making it into a book. The more Josh thought about it, the more he knew he had shared to share it with the world. He would honor Mr. Mac by dedicating the book to him.

It seemed the right thing to do. Then Josh laughed to himself. He thought that by just using a few minutes here and there, he could capture how vital the magic of a moment is to him and possibly others. Mr. Mac would be proud. It is something that should be shared, not kept only to himself.

"This conversation with Peter has reignited my desire to tell the simple truth about the magic of a moment and let others see what can be accomplished in life's moments."

As Josh wrote down an idea about the several ways to put the book together, it started to come to him, and he wrote the ideas down. Funny, he thought, it creates momentum in your life if you take action, even if it is just writing down a thought. The ideas came to mind one after another, and Josh wrote them into his portfolio. When Peter returned to the room, he had almost a full page of thoughts. Josh shut his portfolio as Peter entered the room and sat back in his chair.

"So, I see you have a portfolio, too," Peter said as he sat down.

"Yes, Peter, I sure do. I have had this portfolio for many years. It was a final gift from Mr. Mac, and it is one of my most prized possessions. I can't tell you how many ideas I've captured in it. It's with me always."

"So, it is apparent from just what we have spoken about that Mr. Mac's lesson did its trick with you."

"Yes, it did, Peter. I guess I got hooked on putting things down in writing, just as I did with the other suggestions Mr. Mac gave me. From that day on, I've almost always had something to write down my thoughts. Always! It's amazing how many ideas and thoughts we all have on any given day. If you have a way to write them down, then you can review them later and usually develop further thoughts. It is just a matter of developing the discipline to take the time, the action of writing down what is on your mind."

"It must have been difficult to do that when you were 14 years old. After all, there wasn't a digital way to do things. Writing it down in a note-book, well, must have seemed awkward, didn't it?"

Josh looked at Peter for a long moment and said, "You know, Peter, it wasn't that bad. I wanted to do it, especially as I saw how much you could do if you would write it down. It was like there was something magical about writing things down. It was almost as if it had passed from my mind to the page. Well, it became more real to me. Also, in a way, it begged to be worked on more. It helped me clarify my thinking, which is always a good thing, but more than that, it inspired me to take it further.

"You see, Mr. Mac was wise. He could have given me a portfolio, but instead, he gave me a notepad to keep in my pocket. It was easy to put it in my back pocket and capture an idea here or there as it came to me. At first, when I was walking home that day, I wondered if I would ever have any-thing to write down. Then, it came to me what Mr. Mac had suggested. He told me to write down things I must do and any insights or things I want to do. Anything that came to my mind ended up in my little notepad. I remem-ber going to the back porch of my home. I sat there alone and wrote down what seemed to be a lot. Still, it was only about three or four pages of ideas of things I wanted to do—everything from getting my Chevy to finishing the book I had in my hand. I wrote down things like becoming tight ends on the JV team next year and improving grades. All kinds of things came to me. After a while, I seemed to dry up with ideas and just put them back in my pocket."

Peter smiled and said, "Did you pull it out again?"

"I rode my bike and played baseball with the Williamson boys and Jimmy Fowler. My brothers and I used to play with all the other kids in the neighborhood all the time. They were great fun. During the game, I remember pulling out my little pad and writing down some things I was thinking about.

"It was fantastic to capture all of my ideas and thoughts. It is a habit that I have kept to this day. I think the thing I liked most was not having to worry about things and getting them all out of my head; I didn't worry about losing them. You know, missing an opportunity?"

Josh reached into his pocket and pulled out a small notebook. He lifted it and showed it to Peter.

"This is always with me, Peter; even if my portfolio isn't, this little notebook is where I capture things that come to mind. I guess you would say it's my 'always there' place to take a quick note."

"That is very interesting, Josh, especially when people use digital media so much. So, what Mr. Mac asked you to do really stuck; it made that much of an impact on you, didn't it? You must still see the benefit of having it with you and, more importantly, using it?"

"Oh yes, Peter. Every day of my life, I see the value of it. It's not so much something I have to think about; it's more just the way I live my life. In fact, the ideas for Generation One came as a series of thoughts and insights I had while sitting in a restaurant one afternoon. Primarily because it is just the way I am, I simply took the time to write down some of the ideas that I would like to explore and started to brainstorm about what I wanted and how I might make it happen. I find something very powerful and clarifying about actually handwriting these thoughts."

"Josh, you're telling me that you started Generation One based on simply putting ideas down in your portfolio over lunch?"

"You got it, Peter, I sure did. I know it may seem unlikely, but it's totally true."

"Fascinating, really. It is fascinating how much impact these simple messages have had on you and now our business community."

"Yes, the concepts have had a lot of influence, haven't they? Since I learned this lesson, I developed a series of habits, including always having something to capture my thoughts, that I have used during that time with Mr. Mac that I have kept until this day in my life and probably will for the remainder of my life. I find it easier to make things happen, to get back to my ideas, and to expand upon them when I write them down. It is a great way to think out loud."

"What an interesting way to say it. Is that something you made up?"

"You know, I'm not sure where I got it from, but it works for me," Josh laughed as he said.

"So, what happened when you went back to Mr. Mac?"

"Before I return to Mr. Mac, let me tell you a little about what I experienced that week. I suddenly realized how much was going on in my head and my little teenage world. I didn't believe it. I had countless things I wanted to do or needed to do. The more I wrote, the more came to my mind. I found out that writing them down, like carrying my book, suddenly opened my eyes to the significant number of possibilities all around me. It seemed to be miraculous. But all of a sudden, things I dreamed about and wanted, often something would show up to support them, to make it available for me to have or do. In addition, my world became so much more organized. For the first time in my short life, I seemed to have much more under control. It made me feel more confident, and I knew it was the first step to making something happen. The extraordinary thing was it only took me a moment to write down the ideas or to look them back up. I mean a moment.

"By the way, Peter, that hasn't changed at all. I would write all of this stuff down or look at something on the page and be able to add to it. I found out that most things, as Mr. Mac had suggested in my second lesson, always had smaller, more 'bite-size' parts. I started to write them down and knew if I would get up and do them, remarkable results could occur, and they did. There was something magical about writing them down. Even as a young teenager, I developed the habit of capturing whatever was on my mind. It did seem magical to me, and as a result, my world began to expand.

"That sounds so naive and simplistic, but it is the absolute truth. More than opening up, I knew I could make things happen by capturing the ideas."

Peter looked at Josh for a long time and asked, "Josh, you were changed by these lessons with Mr. Mac. This is so absolutely clear to me. What he asked of you was so simple, yet so profound. I wish I, too, had met a Mr. Mac. A man with that type of knowledge, that type of wisdom could be applicable to all of us. I do appreciate you sharing all of this with me. I know your time is valuable, but I appreciate this type of openness. Your sharing these clear insights with me is perfect. We all need this type of wisdom. I think my readers will also be interested in how these concepts have helped make you the success you are. Please go on."

11

Capturing Ideas

As the conversation between Peter and Josh continued, Josh revealed that Mr. Mac's encouragement to use a small notepad to jot down his thoughts, tasks, and ideas was practical and powerful, increasing Peter's curiosity about the future lessons and what happened as Josh went to meet with Mr. Mac.

Josh admitted that he had been taken aback by the sheer volume of thoughts that filled his notepad. It was a revelation to him, he confessed, that a continuous stream of ideas flowed through his mind, far more than he had ever imagined.

Peter nodded in understanding, acknowledging that most thoughts usually slipped away from their consciousness. He was shocked when Josh revealed that he had filled up his notepad within a week.

Josh explained how the notepad had become a tool for capturing his thoughts, regardless of their magnitude. It was like carrying his book around during his earlier assignment—the tablet catalyzed action, allowing him to document all the random thoughts that were always present in his mind.

Peter found the idea fascinating, and Josh agreed, stating how it had made him realize the sheer number of ideas and questions he had on any given day. He had underestimated this before, he confessed. The notepad had helped him capture countless thoughts, tasks, and questions that came to him throughout the day.

Upon Peter's inquiry about whether Josh had kept all those notes, Josh confirmed that he had every single notepad and even many scraps of paper where he'd written down things.

These notes chronicled his insights and ideas, capturing what he was thinking and wanted to do. They were a significant part of his life.

Peter expressed his interest in practicing this idea, and Josh responded positively. He believed Peter would have a rich trove of ideas and emphasized the importance of reviewing them.

Their conversation then shifted to Josh's next meeting with Mr. Mac. Josh shared how he had arrived at Mr. Mac's house with a new book, *The Hobbit* by J.R.R. Tolkien, and his almost filled notepad. He excitedly told Mr. Mac about how much he had used his notepad.

Mr. Mac was impressed and thanked Josh for taking the assignment so seriously. He also shared with Josh how several brilliant people in history, like Leonardo DaVinci and Thomas Edison, had used notebooks to capture their thoughts and observations.

Josh found this information fascinating and admitted that he initially thought note-taking was only for people who needed help. Mr. Mac assured him it was for everyone and asked about Josh's experience with the assignment.

Josh expressed that it had been a great experience. He felt he could do anything and intended to explore what he could do, enjoy, or have. This new approach empowered him, making him feel in control of his life.

Josh mentioned how beneficial the process had been for him when he spoke to Mr. Mac. Josh mentioned how beneficial the process had been for him. He found it incredibly useful to write down all the thoughts that previously would rush through their mind. He became aware of the numerous things on his mind and how he could make them happen. They became natural to him, not just an idea. Yet, Josh also realized they would only get the chance to do these things if they acted.

He became determined not to let that happen because this was his life. For the first time, he felt like they were genuinely shaping his life the way he wanted it, not just letting it happen to him.

As Josh and Mr. Mac spoke, Mr. Mac commended him for learning this crucial lesson early in life. He explained that everyone has countless opportunities, but most people are either completely unaware of them or only have fleeting glimpses. The key, he said, was first to capture these opportunities and then find ways to make them happen or organize and prioritize them. Mr. Mac advised him to be clear about why they wanted to do certain things, which would help keep them motivated. He also told them not to worry about being unable to get around to everything because life is abundant with opportunities.

When asked how to make sense of all the ideas and tasks he had written down, Mr. Mac reassured them that it was impossible to get to everything. The real key was identifying the essential things and making them a priority. He encouraged him to continue capturing ideas and thoughts, even if he never gets to them.

Josh admitted to having pages of ideas, and Mr. Mac explained how he categorized his notes into immediate tasks, brainstorms, and insights. He defined brainstorming as when one sits and thinks about things, plans how to accomplish something, or considers a way to approach something.

Insights, he explained, were things one noticed that they had never seen before.

Josh agreed with Mr. Mac's definitions and confessed that they had many insights previously considered useless facts. Mr. Mac reassured them that these insights were not meaningless but part of their life's tapestry. He compared the process of capturing thoughts, actions, and insights on paper to focusing a telescope or pair of binoculars—when done correctly, things become clear.

The conversation continued with Josh sharing his idea of starting a small business—a "handyman group" for doing chores around the neighborhood. Mr. Mac commended the view and reinforced the importance of writing down statements as they often take on their own life.

Josh and Ricky, Josh's best friend, agreed enthusiastically and shared their excitement about the countless ways their mind had come up with to make their dreams come true. The conversation ended with them asking Mr. Mac if he had extra time to hear about what happened next.

"Josh, when you write them down, it's as if your dreams and ideas take on a life of their own," Mr. Mac advised.

"Always remember to capture them. They are a part of you, define you, and show what you can contribute to this life.

"Your life is yours to create. Dreams have a way of becoming real, and in a moment, ideas on how to make them happen miraculously come to you, don't they?"

"You're right, Mr. Mac," Josh agreed enthusiastically.

"Suddenly, my mind was full of countless ways to make my dreams come true. It was exhilarating. You can't imagine how I felt. I was overflowing with excitement."

"Tell me about what happened, Josh," Mr. Mac urged, genuinely interested. "I really want to know."

"Of course, Mr. Mac," Josh responded eagerly. "Do you have some extra time now?"

"Josh, it will only take a moment or two," Mr. Mac reassured him. "Of course, I have time to hear what you say.

"Would you like some lemonade? I made some earlier. We could drink it while you tell me about your idea."

"I would love to share my thoughts with you," Josh replied, and the lemonade sounds excellent."

"Let me go fetch it for you," Mr. Mac offered, "and then you can tell me about your ideas. I'll be back in a moment."

12

Making the Most of Every Day

When Mr. Mac returned with their lemonade, Josh promptly expressed his gratitude and enthusiastically began to share his ideas. They discussed possible ways to bring these ideas to life. Mr. Mac, pulling out his portfolio, started jotting down notes.

Josh told Mr. Mac that it wasn't necessary to write everything down, to which Mr. Mac responded that he always made a habit of jotting down his thoughts, as he had once suggested to Josh.

Josh was curious about this habit and asked Mr. Mac why he did it. Mr. Mac explained that writing things down helped him focus better and remember something when he wanted to revisit them later. Josh was impressed by this logic and expressed his admiration for Mr. Mac's practice of what he preached.

As they continued their conversation, Josh shared his excitement about creating something new, especially something as significant as a business. He described how surprisingly easy it felt, likening it to having a blueprint of ideas and thoughts to use. He showed Mr. Mac his notebook, where he had written down his ideas, and began discussing them individually. Mr. Mac asked several insightful questions, which Josh found very helpful.

Josh remarked that writing things down created a sense of Mr. Mac truly listening, which made him feel important and validated his ideas. Peter agreed with Josh, stating that Mr. Mac's attentiveness showed respect for Josh and demonstrated his commitment to understanding Josh's thoughts.

Josh then shared how this experience made him realize the importance of connecting with someone when they are speaking to you, just like Mr. Mac did with him. He mentioned that he now encourages his team to focus on the person in front of them during meetings instead of being distracted by electronic devices.

Peter concurred with Josh's sentiments, emphasizing the importance of being present in the moment, whether learning, listening, or conversing.

Josh agreed with Peter and admitted that he often has to remind himself to be fully present in the moment and not give half attention to something he needs to do or the next thing on his agenda.

The conversation then shifted back to Josh's story with Mr. Mac. He shared how he began to notice changes in his behavior and felt more motivated to act on his ideas the more he wrote them down.

Mr. Mac encouraged Josh to continue this process, emphasizing that while it's impossible to complete all the ideas one has, writing them down and acting on them can lead to countless more possibilities than one could ever imagine.

Josh expressed his hope that Mr. Mac's words would come true and promised to always keep a tool with him to capture his ideas.

Mr. Mac further advised Josh to take time regularly to think about what he wants in life, not just what he wants right now.

Josh was curious if Mr. Mac meant he should do this every day, not just in his free moments. Mr. Mac confirmed this and emphasized the importance of taking time to intentionally plan for what one wants in life.

At this point, Josh was a little apprehensive as this task, which involved quick actions, seemed more challenging than the others. However, Mr. Mac reassured him that it would only take a moment.

Josh reflected on his learning journey with Mr. Mac, realizing that he had learned more from Mr. Mac in a few weeks than he had in nine years of school. He had gained insights about life, how to make a difference, and what was within his control to change.

Peter was intrigued by Josh's story and encouraged him to continue sharing what happened next. Despite needing clarification about his next assignment, Josh determined to carry it out, knowing he could rely on his habit of writing down his ideas.

"Josh, is that the approach you've taken since those early lessons with Mr. Mac?" Peter asked.

"Yes, Peter, that's exactly what I've done. But let's not stray too far from what happened next," Josh responded.

"Please continue, Josh. We have more time, and I'm eager to hear what happened next," Peter said.

"Well, when I asked Mr. Mac to clarify my next assignment, I was somewhat confused. The previous tasks and assignments were straightforward and required immediate action. This time, I actually had to think, which seemed unusual. I was only used to jotting down my ideas, which was very significant to me. I knew I could do that," Josh shared.

"Please continue, Josh," Peter urged.

"Well, Peter, my first question to Mr. Mac was about how and when I should do this," Josh said. "I remember his reaction very clearly."

He recalled how Mr. Mac straightened up in his chair, looked directly at him, and explained, "Josh, it's simple yet specific at the same time. Whenever you have a moment, I want you to write in your portfolio if an idea strikes you, that's not going to change. For the next week, I want you to do something additional. When you wake up in the morning, capture everything you want to achieve in the first few moments. Write down dreams, ideas, and particularly anything that comes to you during your sleep. I know it'll be challenging at first."

Josh admitted to Mr. Mac as a heavy sleeper, which might make this task difficult. However, he promised to try it despite uncertainty about his potential success.

Mr. Mac reassured him, saying, "As you start to capture these ideas, you'll find yourself excited about waking up and getting them down on paper. As we begin to work on things and see them on paper, a certain excitement builds up. Plus, you'll discover a whole new world that you never knew existed."

Josh expressed his trust in Mr. Mac and committed to trying out the new task.

"That's better, Josh. I know you will do it," Mr. Mac encouraged him. As their time came to an end, Mr. Mac reminded Josh to continue working on his earlier assignments and wished him success for the coming week.

Josh thought for a moment and remembered he and Ricky had created a flyer explaining their services. He was very impressed with himself that they had gone to the extra effort to make their first "advertisement of their services."

"Hey, Mr. Mac, would you like one of our flyers?"

"Josh, I would love to have one of your flyers and will look forward to reading it."

"Thanks, Mr. Mac. Here you go." Josh handed the flyer to Mr. Mac with a huge smile on his face.

Josh was thrilled at the prospect of Mr. Mac using their services and assured him they could handle various tasks for him. He thanked Mr. Mac and mentioned needing to leave for a yard job they had scheduled for the day, promising to see him the following week.

13

Daily Intentions

"Peter, allow me to recount all the following week's events," Josh began. "I hope I'm not putting you to sleep, but it was a remarkable week for me. It acted as a pivotal point in my life. It astounds me how such a minor practice could bring about such a significant change. It felt as if all the things I was learning converged and integrated into my lifestyle."

"Of course, Josh, I'm all ears," Peter replied. "From your words, I can tell things were starting to fall into place for you. You might think this isn't of interest to me, but it's quite the opposite. It's astonishing how these fundamental truths and habits influenced your life and everything you've accomplished."

"Thank you for that, Peter. I truly appreciate it. Let's continue," Josh said.

After their conversation, Josh was enthusiastic about his ideas and had several new ones to add. Immediately after their time together ended, he sought out Ricky to involve him in his plans. He shared his thoughts with

Ricky and showed him what he had written down. To his surprise, Ricky was excited about the ideas and believed others would be interested in joining them. Ricky even offered to let Josh have a larger share of any job they secured.

"Peter, you won't believe it, but we had our first job within two days," Josh said. "Mrs. Herbert, who lived down the street from the corner of Berkshire, was our first client. Her husband was always away on business, and she despised mowing her lawn. Ricky and I offered our services to her, explaining our budding lawn mowing business and offering our help. We always provided Mrs. Herbert with the best service since she was our first customer.

"That week flew by so quickly, Peter," Josh continued. "So many things were happening all at once. It was exciting, to say the least, but also a bit overwhelming at times."

"Josh, I'm curious. Did you complete your assignment?" Peter asked.

Josh grinned broadly and replied, "Indeed, I did. In fact, I couldn't wait to get up and start working on it every day. I would literally leap out of bed, go downstairs, sit at the table with my notepad, and jot down what I wanted to do that day. The excitement of the day ahead would often have me rushing out of the house before breakfast! This new routine gave me a type of motivation I had never experienced before."

"Is this still a practice you maintain daily?" Peter inquired.

"Yes, it is, Peter," Josh replied, opening his portfolio to reveal his list for the day. Peter noted the multitude of ideas, thoughts, and plans jotted down on the pages.

"Wow, Josh," Peter said in admiration. "You've really incorporated this into your lifestyle."

"Yes, Peter," Josh responded. "I'm always exploring more things to do and making more connections."

Peter was impressed by how Josh had internalized Mr. Mac's teachings and made them part of his daily routine.

"I did indeed," Josh agreed. "It has been an invaluable lesson and something I strive to practice daily.

"Before our time runs out, let me tell you about the last few lessons Mr. Mac gave me," Josh offered.

"Fantastic, Josh. I'm eager to hear them," Peter said.

"By the way, this is going to make a great article. Thank you for sharing this story with me."

"The pleasure is mine, Peter," Josh replied. "This story changed my life."

14

The Art of Prioritization

Peter could sense Josh's excitement as he spoke of making his way to Mr. Mac's place for their weekly meeting.

Punctual as always, Josh sprinted up the driveway at their agreed-upon time. Mr. Mac was seated on his porch, patiently awaiting Josh's arrival. Despite his many commitments, Mr. Mac appeared unhurried and ready for their meetings.

"Hello, Mr. Mac, how are things?" Josh greeted.

"Everything's great, Josh. Just contemplating a new idea for my house," Mr. Mac replied.

"Really? Your house always seems impeccable. What are you considering?"

"I'm thinking about constructing a greenhouse in the backyard. I enjoy working with plants and watching them flourish, so I believe it would be a nice addition. I'm still in the planning phase, but it seems like a project worth pursuing. Just jotting down a few ideas for now."

"That sounds fantastic, Mr. Mac. Perhaps I can assist you. Ricky and I could lend a hand with moving things around or collecting materials.

We've recently started a business, and although we're getting quite busy and may need additional help soon, we'd be delighted to help you out. It would be a pleasure for us. Just let us know if we can be of any service."

"That's a generous offer, Josh. I'll keep you updated on the progress of my project. Despite our lessons nearing their end, I hope we can continue our weekly discussions.

"How have things been going with your business ideas, Josh?"

"We've secured our first client, and Ricky has joined me in the venture. He was quite taken with my ideas. So we approached our first potential client, and guess what happened?"

"What happened, Josh? I'm eager to hear."

"We presented our services to her, and, believe it or not, Mr. Mac, she agreed on the spot. Just like that, we launched our business. We completed our first job that very day, mowing and trimming her lawn. She was impressed with our promptness.

"We borrowed equipment from our parents to get started—my mom's mower and Ricky's dad's trimmer. We've agreed on a fifty-five to forty-five percent split since the idea was mine. We're working on a flyer to distribute around the neighborhood and estimate we can handle up to twenty yards per week. We're even considering recruiting some friends to help us out. We spent almost two hours last night designing our company's flyer and brainstorming various services we could offer. So, I'm well on my way to getting my truck and, more importantly, launching my first business. Isn't that something?"

"Josh, it's not surprising at all; it's impressive," Mr. Mac responded. "You're developing a true entrepreneurial spirit, which is wonderful. You never know where it will lead you in life. It's these seeds of inspiration that grow and flourish when nurtured properly, which you're certainly doing.

I'm proud of you and the strides you're making. If you remember these steps and apply them consistently, they'll take you far in life."

"I will, Mr. Mac. I know I'll always have questions for you."

"Questions are never a problem, Josh. I'll always be here."

"Thanks, Mr. Mac. I am grateful for the time you've invested in me. I know you're a busy man with a lot on your plate, but you've been incredibly generous with your time. It's made a significant impact on my life already, and I know it will continue to do so. I feel like I'm taking steps towards achieving my goals rather than just daydreaming about them. I feel better about making things happen."

"Josh, that's one of the keys to success. You're taking control and making things happen instead of being a passive participant. Remember, there's always time for what matters most to you. You have to prioritize. For me, spending this time with you is a personal priority. In my small way, I'm making a difference, and that's important to me.

"That's interesting, Mr. Mac. Can we discuss priorities?"

"Of course, Josh. What's your question?"

"Well, since I've been getting up every morning and brainstorming ideas and writing everything down, my folder is overflowing with pictures as soon as they pop into my head.

"They come to me at all times of the day, even when I'm in the shower. Isn't that weird?"

"No, Josh, it isn't. Ideas often come to us when we least expect them, especially when relaxed and stress-free. Please continue with your question."

"Believe it or not, I've even started sketching out my ideas and finding pictures that remind me of something I want to achieve. But there's no way I can accomplish all these ideas. No matter how hard I try, there are always some things I can't get to. Have you ever experienced that? I know you're much more disciplined and organized than I am, but do you ever worry that you won't be able to accomplish everything?"

Mr. Mac gazed at Josh, stating, "Josh, if you execute what we've been discussing and what you've been practicing for the past several weeks, I guarantee you won't manage to finish it all. In fact, just for your information, I never do either.

"I always have an extensive list of things I want to accomplish. Allow me to show you something." Mr. Mac excused himself momentarily, disappearing into the house. After a few minutes, he returned with a small journal, placing it on the table after taking a seat. "Josh, why don't you flip through that journal and see what's inside?"

With anticipation, Josh opened the journal and was shocked by the numerous pages filled with ideas, tasks, and notes Mr. Mac had jotted down.

"Impressive, Mr. Mac; I assumed you stored everything in your portfolio."

"No, Josh, there's not enough paper for that. I sit down and sift through my notes weekly, typically on a Sunday afternoon. I don't necessarily act on most of them, but I like to record the ones I want to 'get to' in my journal. So, every Sunday afternoon, I'm adding new things to it. At the same time, I reviewed it from beginning to end and transferred some of them over to my portfolio for the upcoming week. Does that make sense?"

"Well, Mr. Mac, you always manage to complete what needs doing. It's admirable how you do it without ever seeming rushed or overwhelmed. You even carve out time for me. It's as if you know precisely what you will do every moment. So, you only manage to complete some of your tasks, too?"

"No, Josh, I don't, not even close." Mr. Mac then opened up his portfolio and began to show Josh page after page of pictures, memos, images, and arrows scattered in all directions.

"See, Josh, I have an abundance of ideas, so many I'll never be able to act on. Take a look here; these are some of my notes for my greenhouse project."

"Wow, Mr. Mac. You really don't manage to get everything done, do you?"

"No, Josh, I don't. I realized long ago that if I recorded every thought, sight, aspiration, and obligation, there was no way I could tackle them all. So, I came to understand that prioritization is critical. What's important is doing the things that align most closely with my goals or with what I want to be true in my life."

"I hate to interrupt Mr. Mac, but I like *'what you want to be true in your life.'* I'm going to jot that down and remember it. Please continue, Mr. Mac."

"Thank you, Josh. When deciding how to spend our time, we can begin prioritizing our tasks. It's about saying 'yes' to some things and 'no' to others. Sometimes tough decisions must be made, but that's how we focus on the tasks that matter most to us. It's not just about doing something. It's about doing the right things to create the life you want to live. Does that make sense, Josh?"

"I think so, but how do I figure that out? I mean, when I start looking at things, I think, 'That would be cool to do,' 'That would be great,' 'Oh yeah, I want that too.' Or I think I could make some money doing this or that. Or I think that will be really fun for me. It's a lot. How do I decide what to tackle? You know what I mean?"

"Of course, I understand, Josh. First, you must trust that you've captured everything possible. If you have, you should have a comprehensive list based on the processes we've discussed."

"Yes, that's correct."

"Do you have a reasonably comprehensive list of all the possibilities?"

"Yes, they're all in my little notepad."

"Exactly, Josh, they are. So what do you do in the morning when you wake up?"

"Well, I look at my entire list of things I've written down and start thinking about what I want to do that day and go for it. I sort of figure out what I can fit in, what I can actually get done. Although, honestly, some of them seem pretty urgent to me. I tend to tackle those things first for some reason."

"Yes, and most days, you have much you want to do, more than can be done, correct?"

"Yes, that's why I was asking you about priorities and figuring out what I can do."

"Well, Josh, let me ask you a question. Do you trust that you've recorded everything, and if something new comes up, are you confident you have and will capture those things?"

"Yes, Mr. Mac. No, I'm sure I do."

"Well, having trust in that is incredibly important, Josh. If you know you've recorded everything in your journal as you have done, there are way more tasks than you could complete. Therefore, you'll want to concentrate on tasks you want to ensure get done."

"OK, Mr. Mac, I have my handy journal here. Please tell me the next step. Of course, a lesson comes from all of this."

"Yes, it is indeed a lesson, Josh. So, your next step after you've organized your tasks and thought about them in the morning is to decide what must be done that day. Then, consider the most critical tasks and the items that would be nice to complete if time allows. Of course, if it can be done quickly, get it done. Those tasks would be anything that takes less than five minutes. Get them out of the way. If you do this every day, you'll develop a habit of making time for the most critical tasks. You'll be amazed at the progress you'll make. Remember the tasks you *must do*, the ones that are *most important* to you, and a list of jobs you *might* do. You will also want to have any quick-dos at hand. Is that something you can do?"

"I understand, Mr. Mac. So, focus on must-do tasks and the most critical tasks. Hold off on the might-do items. In short, consider tackling one of the quick tasks."

"Yes, Josh, that's right. I like to allocate specific times for must-do items. In the future, especially when you go to college, you will have many must-do tasks on a calendar. That's the best place for them, too. They need to be done. Most of those tasks are time-specific."

"I might have to get a small calendar for that."

"It's not a bad idea, Josh. It's something you can have and refer to. You don't need to carry it around. You could even sketch out a week on your notepad, with hours marked, and jot down those must-do tasks."

"OK, I got it. Then what do I do with the most critical tasks?"

"First, you should only list three to five of them each day. If you complete the top one, that's a good day. I recommend writing them on a card and keeping them somewhere visible throughout the day."

"So, focus on them whenever I have free time? Got it. I can do that, Mr. Mac. I know I can do it. What happens to the tasks that I don't complete?"

"Excellent question, Josh. I plan on tackling them the next day. OK, Josh, do you know what your next assignment will be?"

"Yes, I do, Mr. Mac. I will go through all of my items on my notepad and then put my must-do tasks on my calendar, which I'll need to get or create. Then, I will go through my list and choose the top items that are most important to me. I will put them on a separate paper and have them with me all day. Will this help me make a choice?"

"Yes, Josh, I believe it will. It would help if you remembered to apply all the earlier lessons and remember those tasks that would be nice. If anything on the list takes less than five minutes, complete it. Can you do that, Josh?"

"I know I can, Mr. Mac."

"That's the spirit, Josh. Remember what I said earlier? What do you want to be true in your life?"

"Absolutely. I'm looking forward to seeing what happens as I do it every day."

"OK, Josh, couple of quick questions. Firstly, where are all of the tasks you might or must do?"

"They're all in my notebook."

"That's right. They're right there, and when you do your quick review—you know, that review that only takes a moment—you can decide whether to move them to the next day or just leave them there for some other time. You see, in that notebook, so much can be captured, and it's always with you, so in those magic moments we all have, you can think about them, move them forward, or simply let them be. Does that make sense to you, Josh?"

"Yes, it does. Is that my assignment for this next week?"

"Yes, it is Josh. I want you to really start thinking about what is most important to you every day. In fact, a good question to continually ask yourself is, 'Is this the most valuable use of my time right now?' Remember, there is always time for what's most important to you. Always. There are some things you might not get to, but make getting to what's most important a priority for yourself."

"That's an excellent point and a thoughtful question, Mr. Mac. If I respond to it honestly, I can see it causing me to reconsider what I might do and how I could utilize my list. Mr. Mac, I'll do it. I'm genuinely curious to see what happens."

"Alright, Josh. As I mentioned, our sessions will soon come to an end. We still have this and a few more assignments to complete. You've been doing wonderfully, and I sincerely hope it's been beneficial for you.

With that in mind, I believe you're prepared to face the upcoming week. Does the same time next week work for you?"

"Mr. Mac, although I must admit that I'll miss our meetings. I've gained so much knowledge, and it's been truly special to me."

"I feel the same way, Josh. See you next week."

"Alright, Mr. Mac. I'm off to play baseball with the guys. See you next week." With that, Josh sprinted towards his bike and pedaled off down the road towards the old field by the church.

15

Purposeful

As one might expect, the week flew by for Josh. He was eager to apply what Mr. Mac had tasked him with. Everything Mr. Mac recommended made a difference, and he was genuinely thankful.

Unexpectedly, during this week, the more he set his priorities and began working, the more he realized he could "make true in his life." He had once heard a quote: "The more you do, the more you can do." It rang true for Josh; he was experiencing that firsthand. The more he worked on his lists and identified what he needed to do, wanted to do, and what would be nice to do, the more his time expanded. He knew it couldn't physically increase; everyone has the same amount of time, but it felt like he always knew what he wanted to do next.

Peter asked, "Is that still the case for you, Josh?"

"Indeed, Peter. I know I can't do everything, but I can accomplish more, especially if I make use of those magical moments we all possess. The magic lies in taking the first step. Even if it's the smallest action, it can make a significant difference. For example, when I need to write something, simply opening the document helps me make progress. Just by initiating it, things start to happen. It's that simplest step that eliminates friction from the equation and invariably leads to progress. I discovered that if I kept my list handy and spent a few moments pondering what I should do and what I might do later, I felt free to take that initial step."

Peter laughed, "That's something I should implement myself, Josh. I often find myself reacting rather than acting with intent. That's what I'm hearing from you—the importance of intentionality.

"Yes, Josh, it's such a simple truth. It's about seizing the moment and taking advantage of each moment's potential. We can do that if we are prepared because of your lessons and have your thoughts and notes readily available. Having it open and reviewing it makes an incredible impact on how you live your life."

"Precisely, Peter. In retrospect, I now understand that Mr. Mac was teaching me to always have clarity about my next steps. He encouraged me to organize them so they were always within my reach. Accessibility is another key. Unbeknownst to me at the time, he was instilling a habit in me that profoundly impacted my life to this day."

"What do you mean by 'accessible' to you?"

"Peter, first and foremost, you need a method to visualize what you want in your life. As Mr. Mac said, you want clarity about what you want to be true. To this day, I still love that statement and truth. That's why physically writing them down is so crucial. You wish to crystalize all of those things you want to be true. The act of physically writing them down holds incredible power. Once written down, they are available. It's as though they are at the forefront of your mind then. But there's more—it allows you to contemplate what you want to be true. Then, you need a system to identify your options and make decisions about them. As Mr. Mac pointed out, you must have a bias towards action. That's what he was teaching me."

"A bias towards action? Could you elaborate on that a bit more, Josh?"

"Certainly, being ready to seize the moments and advance towards those things you want in your life. That intentionality to maximize your life's moments and move forward on the ideas and dreams you want to be true. Our lives are filled with so many opportunities if we take them, but we can't utilize what we're unaware of or haven't captured. Just like these moments we have shared, they have given us time to discuss the magic of a moment and get to know each other better. Moreover, it has allowed me to share something that holds great significance to me. Does that make sense?"

"It does indeed, Josh. It's all coming together and making sense. I've never thought of it in that way, but it's true. You can't do what you don't recognize or, as you put it, have within your reach. It's very true. Plus, having the bias for action you mentioned is also crucial. It starts with that first step, and typically, things start to happen when you take that step, or at least there's a much better chance of them happening. You have no chance to make something happen if you can't remember it or you don't take that first step. It really is a profound truth."

"Peter, I've learned and ingrained the habit of jotting down my thoughts, goals, and insights every day. Not just what I want to achieve but random thoughts about things I want to learn, things I want to consider, or even ideas about something I'm working on. I realize that it can be done in a moment, so I seize those moments of life to make it happen. The very act of intentionally writing down what I want to happen causes significant changes in how I live my life, just as I know it would for anyone. It helps focus our attention on those things that will make the most difference. It also helps elevate our thinking; instead of merely having an idea, suddenly, we're contemplating how to bring it to fruition. Start with the intention and observe what unfolds in the process. You'll find yourself seeking ways to bring the ideas you want to fruition as accurately as possible. At the very least, you'll figure out how to start, which, as I mentioned, is a crucial first step.

"Whether you complete your tasks at that moment, that hour, or that day doesn't matter. The key is to start. It's in the act of creation. Even if it's just writing it down, you break the inertia of passive thought. To me, that's the bias towards action. That's when we want to break the habit of procrastination and start seeing the total value of what we desire. Furthermore, writing it down allows us to begin prioritizing in our minds among all the options we have. We can do so many things, but it begins with intention.

"To sum up, the lessons I learned that week were:

- Dedicate time every day to write down your highest priorities. A few minutes of jotting down your preferences makes a significant difference.

- Spend the first few minutes each day writing down what's important to you.

- Carry your focused list with you throughout the day to check if you're moving from your vision of your day to reality.

"Peter, I believe all of these lessons up to this point with Mr. Mac have enabled me to lead a life of intention. The key is realizing that an intentional life unfolds one moment at a time. For everyone, it's the same—one moment at a time."

By the end of the week, Josh was eager to discuss what he had learned with Mr. Mac.

16

Harnessing the Power of Intention

U pon Josh's arrival at Mr. Mac's residence at their scheduled time, he carried a bunch of flyers and a list of ideas he had been working on.

"Hello, Mr. Mac."

"Hello, Josh. How are you doing?"

"Everything's going fantastic, Mr. Mac. I have quite a lot to discuss with you today."

"I'm excited to hear about it, Josh. Please sit down and fill me in on how things are progressing and the issues you wish to discuss.

"Well, Mr. Mac, I did exactly as you instructed. I must tell you, it felt like a significant week. Suddenly, your lessons started to fall into place."

"I'm eager to hear about it, Josh. What did you learn throughout this week?"

"You might find this cheesy, but taking some time out of your day to think about what matters to you is important. Initially, I was skeptical about how beneficial it would be. However, the more I practiced it, the more value I found in it. Doing it first thing in the morning proved particularly helpful.

It essentially jump-started my day. I found myself contemplating all the tasks I needed and wanted to do, just as you suggested. Moreover, leaving the remaining items on my list in my notebook became less stressful. Does that make sense to you, Mr. Mac?"

"Absolutely, Josh, but why don't you elaborate on it a bit more?"

"I followed your advice to the letter, Mr. Mac. Every morning, I woke up and worked on my list. I knew what I needed to do, but I also started considering what I could do."

"So you practiced this every morning?"

"Yes, I certainly did.

"Simply pausing and asking those questions turned out to be incredibly powerful. It felt like I was suddenly in control of my life, steering it in the desired direction. Does that make sense?"

"It certainly does, Josh. In fact, that's exactly what you were doing. When you start acting with intent, you're deciding how you'll invest your time, money, and effort to create the life you want."

"Well, Mr. Mac, I'm not quite sure about the money part yet, but the time and effort aspects are spot on. Can you further explain the concept of intention?"

"Of course, Josh. Intention is about determining what you want in your life. Think of it as what you want to be true for your life."

"I like that idea, Mr. Mac—what I want to be true."

"That's correct, Josh. Instead of being constantly reactive, you decide what you want to be true and what actions you'll take to make it happen. You begin to live your life intentionally rather than just letting things happen to you."

"That makes a lot of sense, Mr. Mac. My life feels so different now compared to a few weeks ago; it's as if it has meaning now. There's so much more in it—things I didn't even know existed before. It feels complete in a good way. I always have something to do—or rather, I always have things I want to do. It's about acting on things that matter to me.

"I also list things I could do or need to think more about."

"You've hit the nail on the head, Josh. You're making decisions about what you want in your life and the steps you can take to make it happen. Life isn't just happening to you anymore; it's constantly evolving into what you want it to be.

"Does that make sense to you, Josh?"

"It does, Mr. Mac. I now know how to seek the experiences I desire. Plus, with everything I've learned from our lessons so far, I know how to make consistent progress towards realizing them. The magic of life's moments is the gateway to the life I desire. It's astounding how decisive every moment can be when we recognize it."

"That's exactly right, Josh. I really like the perspective you are embracing. You're right—if we recognize the potential in every moment, we can lead much richer lives. It all begins with recognizing those moments are there for all of us and then acting on them, leveraging what we can do *now*. That's the real magic available to everyone.

"So, Josh, why don't you summarize it for me? You've made some remarkable progress. In your own words, tell me what you've learned."

"Alright, let me give it a shot. If I were to sum up what I've learned this week, it would be:

- Take time to think and jot down your most important daily goals. A few moments of contemplation can make a huge difference. It provides focus and clarity.

- Spending the first few minutes of the day writing down what's important to you allows for direction. It stays with you throughout the day, helping you assess whether you're progressing towards what you deem essential in your life."

"That's well-articulated, Josh. You're learning that you have the power to influence and shape your life. It's not left to chance; it's about intentionality. You've learned a lesson that will benefit you greatly. You'll start making remarkable progress if you consistently question what you want to be true in your life or what's missing from it now.

"I can propose a couple of questions for you to ponder as you start your day. Is that alright?"

"Absolutely, Mr. Mac. I'm eager to hear these questions. Let me grab my journal so I can write them down."

"Alright, Josh, here's the first one: What do I want to happen today? As you know, there are far more things on your lists than you can possibly do. By asking yourself this question, you decide what makes the cut for today.

"Does that make sense?"

"It certainly does. In a way, I could do all these things, but these are the ones that will make the most difference in my life right now."

"Exactly. The second question you should ask yourself throughout the day is: What is the best use of my time right now?"

"That makes total sense, Mr. Mac. I like that question. It forces me to decide on the next step, not putting it off, even if I know what I want to do."

"That's correct, Josh. With intentionality, you're adding a sense of urgency. What immediate action can you take to move you closer to your goals? I encourage you to do this throughout your day."

"I love that, Mr. Mac. It's exactly what I need. I like the idea of determining the best use of my time *now*."

"You're right, Josh. What can you do now? The next question you might want to ask yourself is: What are you willing to do to make it happen?"

"Oh wow, Mr. Mac, that's when things get serious. I have to commit to what I'm willing to do."

"You're absolutely right, Josh. It's time to decide what you'll do with all the things in your life. Not just write them down, talk about them, or think about them—what are you willing to do?"

"I assure you, I do need this and will fully utilize this process."

"One last question you might want to consider, Josh: What don't you want in your life, and how can you eliminate it?"

"You'll need to explain that a bit more, Mr. Mac."

"Well, Josh, we've discussed how to get things done and decide what to do, but we must remember that time is not unlimited. Therefore, we must also be equally aware of what we should stop doing."

"I'm not sure I can think of anything like that, Mr. Mac."

"Well, Josh, there might be more things in your life than you realize that you could stop doing."

"Wow, I never considered that before. That sounds like a lesson in itself!"

"Indeed, Josh, you're absolutely right about that. Let's discuss this next week and how you might approach it. Is that alright with you?"

"Absolutely, Mr. Mac. I'm committed to seeing this through."

"I know you are, Josh, and that's why I enjoy working with you on this. Before you leave, let me summarize your assignment for the week: In the morning and throughout the day, ask yourself these questions:

- What do I want to happen today?
- What are the best uses of my time?
- What impact will it have on my life?
- What am I willing to do to make it happen?"

"You got it, Mr. Mac. See you next week. I'm excited to see what unfolds."

17

Reflections on Mentorship

"Josh, your story is nearing its conclusion, I assume. I'm aware we're running against time," Peter acknowledged.

"Peter, this has been quite an enlightening experience. My conversations and learnings from Mr. Mac have influenced me and will interest your readers."

"I appreciate your time, and your words will be helpful to my readers. They are to me," Peter stated.

"The crux of the matter is that my few weeks as a young boy taught me that one of life's opportunities is to give of oneself. Having that bias for action requires just a little energy to take action. The number of opportunities is limitless. Our task is to find ways to perform and proactively approach life. Moreover, it can bring about a change in the lives of others," Josh emphasized.

Josh continued, "One of the guiding principles I've learned is that if you give more than you receive, you'll live a life full of abundance. Giving isn't just about money but also your most precious gift, time. We all can use the moment's magic to embrace this attitude of sharing and giving! How many times could genuinely listening, helping a friend, or simply being there for someone else make a difference? Most of these instances only require a moment and leave you feeling wonderful afterward."

"I've truly enjoyed this, Josh. It's evident how much Mr. Mac meant to you. Two things amaze me," Peter confessed.

"First, that a man like Mr. Mac would take the time to guide a young boy on his journey. It's intriguing that he cared enough to do that. I also wonder if he shared his fantastic insights with others. He must have," Peter speculated.

"Peter, I've often marveled at the same. He did care about me and demonstrated it in countless ways. His insights and teachings are simple yet profound. He took the time to sit with a young teenage boy and share his perspective on life. And it resonated with me," Josh reminisced.

"As for your second question, I often wonder if he did share his insights with others. His teachings impacted me, and I've tried to impart many of these concepts to my team. I constantly encourage them to use the magic of a moment to shape the life they desire and help us build the company we envision," Josh shared.

"Well, Josh, it seems like your team is embracing your teachings," Peter noted.

"Perhaps they are, Peter," Josh agreed.

Peter continued, "The second thing that fascinates me is the profound impact it had on your life. It's so simple and practical, yet it significantly impacted your achievements. What's interesting is that it could work for me, too. Hard for me to believe that you have made a believer out of me."

"It doesn't require a complex system. It just takes action in the next moment before us. In those moments, real magic can occur," Josh explained.

"I can relate to both points, Peter. I was equally amazed that he took time out for me. In today's world, it's rare for someone to invest time in a young person like I was. We don't make that kind of commitment to them. But he did.

"And you're right. It had a profound impact on my life. One moment at a time, it revealed a world to me that I might have missed otherwise. Words can't express my gratitude for him and what he did for me. It truly transformed my life," Josh expressed.

"Okay, let's proceed with what happened with this assignment and the last to come. We still have time," Peter suggested.

"I'm ready if you are, Peter. Please, let's continue," Josh agreed.

18

Taking It One Step at a Time

J osh was a few minutes behind schedule as he hurried towards Mr. Mac's front porch. Mr. Mac was always there, prepared with his aged leather folio and a book.

"Apologies for my tardiness, Mr. Mac," Josh said, "I've been swamped with tasks I want to accomplish. Now that I've listed them all in my journal, I sometimes try to tackle three tasks simultaneously."

"No worries, Josh," Mr. Mac responded, engrossed in his reading.

"May I ask what you're reading, Mr. Mac?"

"Just a book about my hero TR. As you know, he's someone I greatly admire."

"TR? Are you referring to Teddy Roosevelt?"

"Indeed, Teddy Roosevelt is who I meant. He was an extraordinary individual who achieved so much in his lifetime. He's someone I hold in high regard.

"He was a renowned president," Mr. Mac continued, "but I understand he accomplished much more. It's said that he managed to read three books a day and even authored several books during his presidency."

"Is that so?"

"Absolutely, and that's not all. He had this remarkable ability to be fully present in whatever he was doing."

"Fully present?"

"Yes, the ability to focus entirely on the task at hand. If we're distracted, we're not giving our best effort. Sometimes, we need to disconnect from everything else to be in the moment and fully engage in what we're doing."

"That's quite insightful, Mr. Mac. It is exactly the issue I wanted to discuss with you."

"That's great, Josh. Please tell me about your assignment from last week, and we can circle back to Teddy Roosevelt shortly."

"Alright, thank you, Mr. Mac. I did just as you instructed. Every morning, I asked myself what was most important to do and noted them on an index card. I always had three key tasks to do. If I finished them early, I would refer to my list for additional tasks. Secondly, I asked myself what actions I was willing to take that day to make it happen. That's where the real challenge lies, Mr. Mac. It led me to question whether these tasks were important enough to keep me on track. This thought led me to the third question: What can I eliminate to focus on my most important tasks? Does that make sense?"

"It certainly does, Josh," Mr. Mac responded.

The conversation continues between Josh and Mr. Mac as they delve deeper into time management and self-discipline. They discuss the importance of being decisive with how one spends their time and the need to take responsibility for the outcomes one wants in life.

Towards the end of their discussion, Josh expresses his struggle with a huge task that wasn't on his list, but he felt it was the best use of his time.

Mr. Mac shares his approach to such situations: "First, consider what outcome you want from this big task or project. Second, identify the next step you can take towards that outcome. Sometimes, it can be helpful to list one task as 'consider how to make this project happen.' Then, start writing down every idea that comes to your mind, no matter how small."

Josh finds this advice helpful and feels it could help him answer the question, "What is the best use of my time?" more honestly.

"First, Josh, I experience similar situations," Mr. Mac admitted.

"Do you really?"

"Absolutely, everyone does. We all have aspirations in our lives that seem overwhelmingly large. I've trained myself to consider two aspects. First, what do I hope to achieve from this significant task or project? Second, what's the immediate next step I can take towards that goal?

"Occasionally, I list a single task related to the project and ponder how to bring the project to fruition. Then, I jot down every idea that comes to mind. The more minute the detail, the better."

"Does this technique help you overcome roadblocks, Mr. Mac?"

"Indeed, it does, Josh. By doing this, I'm relieving all pressure. I contemplate potential steps toward achieving my goals. When you question what the best use of your time is, you're not just procrastinating, even though you know you should take action. Instead, you're taking a few precious moments to generate ideas on how to make it happen."

"I understand, Mr. Mac. So if that's the honest answer to the question, use those moments to formulate a plan to achieve it."

"Precisely, Josh. You'll be astounded at the outcome if you follow this method."

"I like that idea, Mr. Mac."

"Wonderful. Were there any other obstacles that prevented you from answering that question?"

"Yes, Mr. Mac, there were. Several times, I knew the answer was to complete a small task that had either just arisen or was something I didn't deem necessary to include in my daily list."

"I see, Josh. So it was a minor task that you knew if you completed promptly, it would be off your mind and accomplished."

"Yes, Mr. Mac. It's funny how, if I didn't complete it, it kept circling in my mind. I spent more time pondering it than actually doing it."

"I understand, Josh. This is a common occurrence for everyone. I have a practice that works effectively for me. If there's a task that can be completed instantly or within a few minutes, I do it immediately. It might not be on your daily list, but it's still something to have true in your life, correct?"

"Yes, Mr. Mac. Often, they hardly take any time at all."

"I completely understand, Josh. Consider it as a break from your planned day. You can allocate 15 minutes to tackle a couple of tasks or decide that it's a good use of your time to complete it now so it's off your mind and you can concentrate on your other crucial tasks.

"Would that be helpful for you, Josh?"

"You know what, Mr. Mac? It might be quite beneficial. Both of these ideas are excellent and would allow me to answer the question honestly."

"I agree, Josh. You've taken this assignment very seriously, and I'm impressed."

"Thank you, Mr. Mac. I really delved into it. It was intriguing how full my days were without feeling any pressure."

"That's wonderful, Josh. So you accomplished a lot?"

"Absolutely. I probably achieved more this week than I ever have in a week. It's exhilarating. It feels fantastic to be on top of things that I need to do, but more importantly, to be doing the things that truly matter to me, things I want to be a reality in my life."

"That's fantastic, Josh. I couldn't be more pleased. Let's dedicate more time today to discuss your next assignment. Given what we just discussed, it would be ideal. You only have two more projects, and I'm certain you'll find relief."

"Mr. Mac, I'm learning so much. These lessons are truly transforming my approach to life, and I love it. I can't wait for the next assignment. Did I just say that?"

"You certainly did, Josh. Let me grab a glass of lemonade, and we can discuss the next assignment."

"Sounds great, Mr. Mac. Thank you."

19

Reflecting on the Magic of Moments

"Well, Peter, have you had enough yet?"

"No, I haven't, Josh. I will let you know.

"I can't help but think about how these concepts apply in my own life, which is not very good boundaries for a reporter, but the truth. I'm so struck by the practical common sense of these assignments and wonder why we aren't taught this more clearly early in life. It would help so many people to know this information," Peter shared with Josh.

"I think so, too, Peter. I never learned any of this in school. But as I think about it, if we instructed students on these practices earlier in life, what amazing things they could achieve. It would help students, and it's even excellent advice for adults."

"Yes, it is Josh. I'm intrigued by your question, 'What is the best use of my time now?' It's such an important question. It was for you and one you took very seriously in your conversation with Mr. Mac."

"It's true, Peter. That particular question is my centering and grounding question."

"What do you mean, Josh?"

"Well, during my day, and I imagine for many others, we just get caught up in the flow of the day. That's great in some ways, but it can often leave us in a reactive mode. We get to the end of the day and can't remember anything that happened. Does that make sense?"

"Yes, Josh, it does. It happens to me all of the time. Could you say more about it?"

"Sure, when we are 'caught up' in our day, we are all thinking about the next thing we are doing or avoiding. When we ask this question—What is the best use of my time now?—something magical happens. When I ask that question, it centers me on the moment. It allows me to pause to consider how I want to use my life's energy. At that moment, I'm back in my life, not living externally to the day's happenings, putting me on firm ground again."

"I can see that, Josh. There is an immediacy to it, isn't there?"

"Yes, very much, Peter. At that moment, the world seems right. I am back in control, making decisions, not just reacting."

"Do you still do this, Josh? Do you still ask the question?"

"Yes, I do, Peter. In many ways, it's more important now than ever in my life. As you develop more demands on your time, you can more easily be swept away by the various tasks and 'things to do' around you."

"I can sure relate to that, Josh."

"I know. It is probably true for everyone. For me, my mind is always coming up with ideas. In that moment of centering, that precious moment, I can get my bearings again and make a deliberate decision about my time and, for that matter, my life. It is very empowering, to be honest. Also, it would help if you thought it was about something other than creating something, doing something, or being productive. Sometimes, the best use of my time is to relax, reconnect with a friend or colleague, or chill out. I never thought about the non-work parts of my life being a decision, but it is.

"Yes, it is Peter. It's one of the great lessons Mr. Mac taught me. It stays with me in significant ways."

"Josh, this is helpful to me personally. Thank you. Do we still have time to finish the story?"

"Yes, we do, Peter. It would be my pleasure. I was curious about what my next assignment would be. I knew we were coming to an end of learning about the magic of a moment, so I was anxious to hear what Mr. Mac would say."

"I bet, Josh. It was clear he had a plan and knew how this might all progress for you, which I find entirely intriguing."

"Yes, he did, Peter. So, let's see where I was. Mr. Mac returned to the porch with lemonade for both of us. It tasted so good; August in Florida can be brutal, and cold lemonade hit the spot for us both.

"As he sat down and we began sipping our lemonade, he said, 'Josh, are you ready for your next assignment?'

'Yes, I am Mr. Mac. I'm excited to see what is next. I'm sad that our lesson time is ending.'

'Me too, Josh, but we can discuss any questions or other things anytime.'

'That is great, I would like that a lot. I'll have questions even after our lessons.'

'Of course, Josh, it would be my pleasure anytime. Let's talk about a critical concept: review.'

'Review?'

'Yes, review Josh. Review is a way to process what is happening in your life. Not just reacting to life but being very conscious of what you are making of your life. As we said before, are you progressing on what you want to be true in your life?

'Review is a time dedicated to centering ourselves and asking if we live the life we want. It's an act of looking backward and forward.'

'What do you mean by that, Mr. Mac?'

'Well, Josh, we can learn from history what is happening in our lives. Our lives as we live them leave cues if we only take the moments necessary to notice them. We all have outcomes for everything we do, some good, some bad. We can learn a lot from both.'

'What do you mean about learning from the bad? Do you mean when we fail at something?'

'Yes, Josh, in a way. These things are not failures; they are just the result of something we did that didn't get the desired outcome.'

'I see, Mr. Mac, that makes sense.'

'Great Josh. As we live our days, we have all kinds of outcomes or goals for what we do. We do this so, as we said before, something can be true in our lives. Right?'

'Yes, that is why we are doing them.'

'Exactly, Josh, and many times we are successful, but sometimes we aren't. Whether we achieve the outcome we want or not, it provides feedback.'

'What do you mean by feedback, Mr. Mac?'

'Well, Josh, we sometimes do things that get us exactly what we want. In other words, what were the things we did that helped us be successful in achieving our intention? Does that make sense to you, Josh?'

'Yes, it does. That one seems easy to see.'

'It is easy to see, but we need to take the time to pause and consider what occurred. It is so valuable. We can learn much from it and see how we can move forward. In other words, it confirms what we will do in the future from what we learned and how we might change.

'Josh, we can learn much from this, especially when we still need to achieve what we want.'

'Please explain that a little more, Mr. Mac. I understand, but this is new for me. Most of the time, I only take a little time to review what I did. I get onto the next thing.'

'Most people do that, Josh, but the act of review, or you might think of it as reflection, allows us to see what is happening. It's tough to do when we are in the middle of something. We become consumed with whatever it is we are doing. We keep perspective if we regularly review what is happening during the day, at the end of the day, and even once a week.'

'Perspective, Mr. Mac?'

'Yes, Josh, perspective. I like to think of the attitude of making something visible in our mind and being able to examine it and think about how it fits into my life. The reviews we are discussing allow us the opportunity to do just that.'

'I see, Mr. Mac. I like the idea of pausing and also the value of reflecting. Honestly, I rarely do it, though.'

'As I said, Josh, most people don't, but I want you to try it.'

'I will, Mr. Mac.'

'Before I give your assignment, please let me share an important quote with me regarding reviewing.'

'I would love to hear it, Mr. Mac.'

'Great, it comes from an Ancient Greek Philosopher, one of the truly great thinkers of all time. His name was Socrates. Have you ever heard anything about him?'

'I've heard about him, Mr. Mac, but I don't know anything about him.'

'Well, Socrates was a great thinker. This particular quote is attributed to him when he was on trial for his life or the chance of exile. Socrates believed that philosophy—the study of wisdom—was the most important pursuit we could ever take. For some, he exemplifies more than anyone else in history the pursuit of knowledge through questioning and logical argument, examining, and thinking. His "examination" of life in this way spilled out into the lives of others. In many cases, they often began their own "examination" of life. Still, he knew they would all die one day, as he said that a life without philosophy—an "unexamined" life—was not worth living.'

'Wow, Mr. Mac, that is so cool. It is. He was a great thinker, wasn't he?

'So, what is the quote, Mr. Mac?'

'It is: "The unexamined life is not worth living."' He further explained Socrates' philosophy and his belief in the importance of examining life. He emphasized how this quote was especially relevant to the concept of review.

The quote and its profound implications deeply moved Josh. He understood why Mr. Mac frequently thought of it, especially about reviewing. He could see how the practice of review and quote was life-changing, prompting anyone to pause, review, reflect on their lives, and continually realign their lives based on this reflection.

"That is impressive, Mr. Mac," Josh stated.

"Indeed, it is, Josh. Can you see why I think about it so frequently, particularly when we consider what I'm requesting you to do with the review?" Mr. Mac asked.

"I sure can, Mr. Mac. It's really amazing to me how such a brief quote can hold so much power," Josh replied.

"It's transformative, Josh. Taking a moment to pause, review, and reflect on what's transpiring in your life ensures you don't lead an unexamined life. We constantly take time to realign our lives through this reflection," Mr. Mac explained.

"Mr. Mac, how does this align with the concept of the magic of a moment?" Josh asked, intrigued.

"Everything I've guided you towards is meant to empower you to take control of your life. This concept of reviewing and leading an 'examined' life allows you to steer in the direction you desire. It provides an opportunity to re-center yourself on the path *you* are determining for your life, not just what is being dictated externally for you," Mr. Mac clarified.

"Does that make sense to you, Josh?"

"Yes, Mr. Mac, it indeed does," Josh replied.

"Excellent, Josh. Now, I have a task for you this week. It won't be too demanding, but I assure you it'll make a difference," Mr. Mac proposed.

"Alright, Mr. Mac."

"The first task is for you to set aside some time on Sunday to sit down and review what has transpired during the week. Reflect on your experiences and your journal entries. Contemplate something you learned from these experiences. "Then, think about the upcoming week and what you'd like to accomplish. Be very specific about when you'll do them, the physical activity involved, and what will be necessary," Mr. Mac explained.

"Do you think you can handle that, Josh?"

"Yes, I can do that, Mr. Mac. It will be intriguing to see what I uncover during that time. I appreciate the idea of reflecting on what I've done and what I plan to do. It will allow me to really discover if I'm heading in the direction I want and how I could adjust my course for the next week," Josh responded enthusiastically.

"Exactly, Josh. In those moments of review, you can guide your life. Like everything in life, sometimes we need to make adjustments. This process allows you to contemplate them and adjust as necessary," Mr. Mac affirmed.

"Thank you, Mr. Mac, I can do that. You mentioned this was my first task. Is there another?" Josh asked.

"Yes, Josh, there's another task with the same theme but of equal importance. At the end of every day, please take a few minutes to review what you've accomplished and ask yourself how it aligns with your morning priorities. Does that sound reasonable to you, Josh?" Mr. Mac instructed.

"Yes, Mr. Mac, that sounds like an excellent idea. If I spend time during the day thinking about what I want to accomplish, it's equally important to check if I actually achieved what I set out to do. I guess, in a way, I'll be having a conversation with myself," Josh reasoned.

Mr. Mac chuckled. "Yes, Josh, you would be. Spending a few minutes at the end of the day is an act of integrity to me."

"Integrity? I've heard that word, but could you elaborate on it for me?" Josh asked.

"Of course, Josh. Living with integrity means living your life consistently with the values and beliefs you hold inside you, moment by moment. In every moment, we all have the opportunity to live in alignment with what we say we want in our lives or not," Mr. Mac explained.

"I see, Mr. Mac. The daily and weekly reviews allow you to assess if you're being true to what you're saying and what you believe internally," Josh reflected.

"That's exactly right, Josh. Can you tell me why it's so important to do this daily and weekly?" Mr. Mac asked.

"Yes, I think so, Mr. Mac. Sometimes, if we reflect on what we did that day, we might remember what actually happened. It's so closely tied to how we started our day that it can still be fresh in our minds. I bet it's a lot more powerful when it's still new to us, isn't that right, Mr. Mac?" Josh pondered.

"Yes, great answer and precisely on point, Josh. When you do your daily review, you can see if what you planned not only transpired but also think about how you could do it differently in the future and any learnings from it. It's a matter of having more immediate feedback," Mr. Mac confirmed.

"I can see that, Mr. Mac. That way, I can determine if I'm just spinning my wheels," Josh responded.

"That's correct, Josh. I do both of these things that I'm asking you to do and even add one more," Mr. Mac revealed.

"What's that, Mr. Mac?" Josh asked.

"Josh, I always try to have that end-of-the-day review during the day, just as I'm asking you to do. Another thing I do is capture thoughts during the day as I finish what I've been doing and write down what I want to do next. It's like a pause, capturing immediate thoughts about my previous experience and also having a chance to plan the next," Mr. Mac explained.

"That sounds like a lot, Mr. Mac, but I can see how that would be valuable," Josh acknowledged.

"Do you want to know the best part about it, Josh?" Mr. Mac asked.

"Yes, what is that, Mr. Mac?" Josh responded eagerly.

"It only takes a moment. I've gotten to where I can do this in just a moment. I often review everything I've captured for my end-of-the-day review and re-read all of the items as I take stock of the prior week during my weekly review," Mr. Mac shared.

"Mr. Mac, I want to try that, too, this week. It might be helpful for me. Doing something so immediate could help me reflect on what I did and what I can do in the future," Josh agreed.

"Alright, Josh, you have your assignments. Our time is ending, but I'm impressed with how you've embraced these concepts and tasks," Mr. Mac praised.

"Thank you, Mr. Mac. These concepts are making a significant difference in how much I accomplish and how I feel about myself. I'm actually directing my life in the direction I want. It's a great feeling," Josh shared.

"I'm delighted to hear that, Josh, and I can see it happening for you. I'm genuinely happy for you," Mr. Mac expressed.

"Thank you, Mr. Mac. I will do my best," Josh promised.

"Alright, Josh, see you at the same time next week," Mr. Mac bid farewell.

"You can count on it, Mr. Mac. I'll be here. Until then, have a great day," Josh replied.

20

Staying on Course

"Well, Peter, I left that particular meeting, especially since it was one of my last. I was sad and wondered how it would help me now and in the future."

"It seemed like a lot, Josh, but it made sense to me as he explained it to you. I've never actually thought about it that way. I get caught up in what I have to do today."

"That was true for me too, Peter, even as a teenager. It could be how it is for me now, except for this practice."

"Do you still do it, Josh?"

"I sure do, Peter. Every Sunday afternoon, I take time to do what I call my extensive review."

"Wow, did it stick with you that much?"

"It sure did. I have gotten into the practice of looking at what happened in the past week. I want to reflect on what happened, but I also wish not to kid myself if I lived the life I wanted to live."

"I don't think many people do that, Josh. Most are stuck in that 'next' thing, whatever it is, or just surviving."

"I agree, Peter, but Mr. Mac was onto something. If we don't stop and reflect, even a little, on our week, we tend to repeat it the following week. Does that make sense?"

"Yes, it does, Josh. It goes back to Socrates, the unexamined life."

"So true, Peter, so true. So, it became a practice. I didn't stop there. I also look at what is true right now. I think about where I am with my day and re-orient myself if needed. I like to think of it as using a map. I've already figured out where I've been by what we discussed; now is the time to understand where I am and determine if I'm still on the right course."

"How do you do that, Josh?"

"Peter, I look through my lists and think about every item."

"Every item?"

"Yes, every item. It makes me feel on top of things when I do that. Plus, I often end up eliminating things or scratching through them. It may have been a possible idea or task when I wrote it down, but now it's unimportant to where I want to go and be."

"That makes complete sense to me, Josh."

"Yes, Peter, it is something I continue to do. I typically look through my journal writings and now my notes on my computer."

Josh went on to say the process allows him to have a perspective to work from. "I think about what I must do, but I also think about what I want to do."

"What happens when you do that?"

"Well, two things. First, I develop a plan for the week.

"I come up with those things I must complete and calendar those must-dos."

Peter asked, "So, you put it on your calendar?"

"Yes, I sure do, Peter. If it is a must-do, it goes on my calendar. It is the best place for the must-do items."

"What do you do with the things you may want but have yet to do?"

"Great question, Peter. I have them on a list that is with me always. Let me show you." Josh pulls out a notecard with bullet points on it.

"So that card is the thing you want to do for this week."

"Yes, it sure is."

"It's full of items."

"Yes, Peter, it is, but you would be surprised how often I get them all done, even with quite a few must-haves in my life."

"Is this why you are so productive?"

"It contributes to it, but more than anything, it focuses on what I want and is important to me. Then, the moments appear in my life almost by magic, and I can take action."

"The bias for action, right?"

"Yes, Peter, I can get so much done by using these concepts and just taking a step. It's still genuinely unique to me, but as if, again, the moments appear to me by magic.

"The thing is, I would have never known about them or certainly remembered them if I hadn't written them down and made them accessible. It's funny. To me, it's like a superpower. It is very motivating if it is important to you and you have confirmed that it is what you want to happen.

"You seek time to make those things happen, and this flood of energy rushes out to meet you and leads you to take action."

"You know Josh, I can see that."

"It is, Peter. We can all dream, and we can all talk about what we want in our lives. That said, what is important is how you use these precious moments of your life and take full advantage of them."

"Well, that gives me a lot to think about Josh. Something else emerges from the practice."

"What's that, Peter?"

"Well, trust. You trust the process, and because you do, you can commit to it."

"That is precisely right, Peter. Well, I am said. That trust in the process frees me to engage in those things I say are important. I do it without hesitation and have a deep conviction that I'm moving in the direction of the life I want. There is a sense of completeness when I do it."

"What do you mean, Josh?"

"I know what I want to do for the next week, the things I want to accomplish. In addition, I can let go of the other things I have in my notes or might want to do. Does that make sense?"

"It does, Josh, but they need to be completed."

"True, Peter, but I commit to completing them in my mind.

"It's not something I'm thinking about anymore. It's something I'm going to do."

"So when you come up with your list, it's a genuine commitment."

"Exactly. I can't tell you how freeing it is for me. I will have to take time to do other items, but I do it without hesitation. None. I'm committed to making it happen."

"That makes total sense to me now, Josh. So you had two assignments, though. You would do a daily review and, even during the day, do a shorter, immediate review."

"Yes, that is true, Peter. I will tell you it is equally powerful for me."

"So you did it, too?"

"Oh yes, Peter. In many ways, this is equally meaningful for me. I use what I come up with during those reviews in my Big Review. The immediacy of those reviews provides me with clear feedback I can use to test myself with a sense of integrity."

"What do you mean by 'integrity'?"

"Peter, you can say something is essential, but what do you have if you don't act on it? It's not what you say, what you plan for, or what you write down. It comes down to what you do."

"You got it, Josh. It makes sense to me. You can mislead many people, but you can't lie to yourself."

"That's how I see it, Peter. I want to be true to what I say I will do and make it happen. Plus, a keen awareness stays with you during the day and forces you to answer the question honestly: Is this the best use of my time?"

"So, a hyper-awareness of your actions."

"Strictly, I have repeated daily opportunities to take stock of what is happening and course correct if necessary. Plus, doing those short reviews moves me forward with a new awareness of adjusting and adapting to make what I want to happen."

"Please talk about that."

"Sure, when I do the end-of-the-day review and the mini-reviews during the day, I will often look at what happened.

"How much time have I taken to do it? What helps me effectively do it? Is there a particular context that is needed for it to happen? Are others important to make it happen?"

"It sounds like a powerful way to look at your day," Peter shares.

"Yes, it is, and to me, it empowers my day."

"Oh, so it also continually motivates you?"

"Yes, it does. Once I review it, I can move forward and take the learning and motivation to whatever I intend to do next."

"That is great. So, how did it go with Mr. Mac when you reported on the week?"

"Let me tell you about that and the last assignment. We can get it in before the night's activities."

"I appreciate that, Josh. I'm looking forward to hearing it."

21

Harnessing the Magic of Moments: Reflection, Intention, and Progress

Josh arrived at Mr. Mac's home slightly late, apologizing for his delay and explaining that he had been conversing with Ricky about their work.

Mr. Mac assured him it was not an issue, as he had been engrossed in his project, and Josh was only a few minutes late.

Curious, Josh asked about the project Mr. Mac was working on.

Mr. Mac revealed he was working on some vocabulary words, specifically Spanish.

Surprised, Josh asked if Mr. Mac spoke Spanish.

Mr. Mac confessed that he did not yet speak Spanish but was utilizing his time to learn new words.

Impressed, Josh expressed his desire to learn another language but admitted that he was struggling enough with English.

Mr. Mac found Josh's comment amusing and encouraged him, asserting that Josh could indeed learn another language.

Skeptically, Josh questioned how he could achieve this, as he wasn't enrolled in any language classes at school.

Mr. Mac offered to show him a method requiring only a moment.

Josh complimented Mr. Mac on smoothly incorporating the magic of a moment concept into their conversation.

Mr. Mac agreed but shifted the conversation, asking about Josh's week.

Josh enthusiastically shared that his week had been outstanding. He managed to conduct the Big Review once and found it enjoyable.

Mr. Mac appreciated the term "Big Review" and inquired when Josh had conducted it.

Josh revealed that he had done it on Sunday afternoon, recognizing that it was an ideal time before starting his week.

Mr. Mac agreed, stating that Sundays were a perfect time for reflection on one's life and past events.

Josh concurred, sharing that this method had worked well for him.

Mr. Mac then asked for more details about what Josh had done.

Josh explained that he had referred to his journal and was surprised at the amount of information he had noted and subsequently forgotten.

Mr. Mac assured Josh that this was a shared experience and one of the reasons for conducting the review.

Josh expressed his understanding and shared how he had initially been unsure about the assignment's benefits.

However, as he conducted it, he realized its importance and felt liberated.

Mr. Mac asked for further clarification on this feeling.

Josh elaborated that as he revisited his notes, he remembered why he had written them and how they could be utilized multiple times. This process made him feel free and energized.

Mr. Mac agreed, stating that reflection brought freedom to everyone as it allowed them to incorporate their experiences into their lives.

Josh affirmed this sentiment, sharing that he had completed his tasks and felt liberated by the ability to move forward.

Mr. Mac encouraged Josh to continue sharing about his process.

Josh explained that after reviewing everything, he ended up noting down several other things as a result. He jokingly referred to the magic of a moment concept as he mentioned how quickly he could capture these ideas.

Mr. Mac laughed heartily at this, complimenting Josh on his excellent use of the concept.

Josh then shared how he contemplated everything in his life and what he anticipated for the upcoming week. He had noted everything for the week on a sheet in his journal.

Mr. Mac commended Josh and suggested that as more things occurred, he should keep a calendar to note down all his must-do tasks.

Josh pointed out that he only had a few scheduled tasks.

Mr. Mac reassured him that he would in the future and could schedule things he wanted to do for now.

Josh questioned if he could schedule just anything he wanted to do.

Mr. Mac confirmed this, explaining that he could carve out what he wanted to happen in his calendar to ensure it fit into his life.

Josh appreciated this idea and promised to implement it.

He then discussed how he had determined what he wanted for the week and noted it in his journal, asking if he could show Mr. Mac.

Mr. Mac agreed, eager to see it.

Josh showed Mr. Mac his journal, revealing his list of desired outcomes for the week.

Mr. Mac praised Josh for his comprehensive list.

Josh agreed but mentioned a strange occurrence.

Curious, Mr. Mac asked what it was.

Josh shared that as he went through the week, he found himself using bits of time to work on the tasks on his list, attributing this progress to the magic of a moment.

Mr. Mac explained that this was the intended outcome. By capturing these tasks during the review, they remained at the forefront of Josh's mind and became accessible whenever needed.

Confused, Josh asked what Mr. Mac meant by "accessible."

"Josh, having your thoughts and reflections accessible means they aren't hidden within your journal pages or your thoughts. They have been made available to you on this page you are showing me," Mr. Mac explained.

Surprised, Josh admitted, "Wow, I didn't think of that, Mr. Mac. You know what? I can totally see it. It's like a constant reminder that's always with me."

"That's right, Josh," Mr. Mac affirmed, "The more you contemplate them during your review, the more you realize that they are accessible and can be used to progress. Having them readily available as you do now is a powerful concept and learning experience for you."

Josh agreed, expressing curiosity about how he managed before incorporating reviews into his routine.

Mr. Mac responded with a thought-provoking statement, "Most people in this world go about their lives without really contemplating their potential, let alone having it documented on a page right in front of them. When you do, it motivates you to seize the countless moments that surround us every day."

Josh resonated with this, sharing his personal experiences from the past week that validated Mr. Mac's statement.

Mr. Mac then praised Josh for his dedication to the assignment given for the week. Josh expressed his gratitude and commitment to applying the lessons he had learned from Mr. Mac indefinitely.

Mr. Mac was confident in Josh's resolve and urged him to share his experiences with the second assignment.

Josh was enthusiastic about the impact this assignment had on his life.

Intrigued, Mr. Mac asked for specifics.

Josh explained how the assignment had transformed his routine and thought process. He shared his experience of taking a "moment" at the end of each day to review all that had transpired and how this practice was greatly enhanced by what he did during the day.

Mr. Mac asked for more details.

Josh described how he would take a moment to capture a thought or two as he transitioned from one task to another.

He would note down his feelings about what he had just done, whether positive or negative, which often led him to think of other tasks he needed to do or changes he wanted to implement.

Mr. Mac found this exciting and pointed out that pausing to reflect on one's actions can become a learning experience.

Josh agreed and shared how he found jotting down these quick thoughts very beneficial.

When asked how it was helpful, Josh explained that it allowed him to set aside the current task and move on to the next one. He would often make a note of what he planned to do next.

Mr. Mac understood and pointed out two fundamental concepts that Josh was implementing: learning from experiences and approaching tasks with intent.

Josh affirmed this, recognizing that every experience can teach us something if we take a moment to think about it. Mr. Mac elaborated on this, explaining that when Josh paused, he was achieving closure on what he was doing and allowing himself to move forward. He also suggested that this pause might unconsciously enable Josh to celebrate taking action.

Josh understood this concept, realizing that the closure and celebration were happening unconsciously.

Mr. Mac confirmed this and introduced another concept: engaging the intention muscle.

When asked to explain, Mr. Mac described how Josh intentionally decided what would be true every time he took a moment to reflect on the past and plan for the future.

Josh questioned how this was a muscle. Mr. Mac explained that each time Josh acted on his intentions, he was strengthening his self-discipline and realizing his ability to achieve what he wanted.

Josh was amazed by this perspective and recognized why he felt a surge of energy. He understood that repeated practice of this would make him more assertive in acting on his desires.

Reflecting on his week, Josh realized how much he had accomplished and acknowledged the Magic in these moments. He also recognized how this practice had helped him determine the best use of his time.

Mr. Mac agreed, stating that Josh was tapping into his power to prioritize what was essential to him, which felt empowering.

Josh described it as a rush, realizing that he could make anything happen if he took action, even if it were a small step.

Mr. Mac agreed and asked if there was anything else Josh had learned from the second assignment.

Josh shared how effortless it was to do in the evening, as all he had to do was review what he had written down during those brief moments. He expressed surprise at how much he could accomplish in a day, which motivated him to continue this practice.

Mr. Mac was delighted with Josh's experience and looked forward to discussing the last assignment.

22

The Power of Kaizen: Small Steps Towards Massive Change

A s one might expect, this was a pivotal lesson for Josh.

He derived immense value from it.

Observing Josh's enthusiasm, Peter shared his insights: "I can see that, Josh, and I've learned a lot from this myself. I never take the time to ponder what's happening during my day to realize that I can do that with just a moment of thought. It's quite impactful. I can't fathom why more people don't know or practice this."

Josh agreed, emphasizing the potential benefits for everyone.

Peter, curious about Josh's interactions with Mr. Mac, inquired about their initial meeting when Mr. Mac was learning Spanish and asked about Josh's last assignment.

Josh was more than willing to share his experiences.

Peter acknowledged the profound impact these experiences had on Josh's life.

Josh agreed and proceeded to recount his remaining time with Mr. Mac.

During one of their conversations, Josh asked Mr. Mac about his continuous learning habits, "So Mr. Mac, since we have talked about this last assignment, can we discuss what you were doing when I first met you and you were learning Spanish? I was stunned, well, that you are still learning. Do you do that every day?"

Mr. Mac confirmed, "Yes, Josh, I do. A long time ago, I decided to use my moments during the day to continuously learn and grow as a person."

Josh found this impressive and shared the misconception that learning ends after formal education.

Mr. Mac clarified that while interest plays a role in learning, there are countless opportunities for growth if one chooses to seize them. He emphasized the importance of using life's moments for self-improvement and development.

Josh was intrigued by the idea of limitless learning.

Mr. Mac confirmed this possibility and introduced Josh to the concept of Kaizen.

Josh was unfamiliar with the term Kaizen.

Mr. Mac explained that Kaizen is a Japanese word that means "change for the better," and it results from numerous minor improvements. These incremental gains accumulate and lead to significant results over time.

Josh appreciated this concept as a comprehensive encapsulation of positive change.

Mr. Mac agreed and further explained how the idea of Kaizen went beyond simple addition, implying exponential growth. He illustrated how Kaizen could apply to individuals just as it does to organizations. He described the "compound effect" at work, where many small, repeated gains lead to significant change.

Josh was fascinated by the potential of utilizing small blocks of time for substantial life improvements.

Mr. Mac confirmed this potential and its future implications.

Josh pondered over another aspect of this concept—commitment.

Mr. Mac agreed that commitment was vital to the process.

He explained how understanding this concept naturally draws one towards incorporating it into one's life.

Josh wanted to know how to make and integrate such a commitment into his life.

Mr. Mac saw this as an excellent transition into Josh's final assignment and prepared him for it.

23

Embracing Kaizen in Daily Life

"Are you prepared to hear about my final task, Peter?"

Peter had a reasonably clear idea of Mr. Mac's direction with Josh.

"Yes, me too; I had already learned so much from him. It was sad to be finishing up," Josh added.

"I bet it was. I would very much like to hear about the last assignment.

"I think we can manage it within our remaining time. After that, I'll have to head to the stage for the final instructions," shared Josh.

"Let's proceed then, Josh."

Mr. Mac looked at Josh and said, "Before we delve into the final task, let's revisit the first six tasks you've completed to reach this point. I want to illustrate how each contributes to integrating Kaizen into your life. Committing to this final task will serve as a guiding force for maximizing your life potential.

"So, Josh, let's begin with the first task. Could you remind me what it was?"

"Certainly, Mr. Mac. It was about taking out the garbage," he quipped. "Just kidding. The first task taught me to act immediately and not procrastinate or delay things. The act of taking out the garbage was a metaphor for this lesson.

"It taught me to act promptly, thus preventing unnecessary dwelling on it in my mind. In many cases, tasks can be completed in mere moments."

"Well done, Josh. It truly is a fundamental skill. To have the life you desire, you must be willing to act on what you need or want to do. Moreover, most things in our lives can often be acted upon and completed in just a moment. It's indeed a foundational skill. So, Josh, what was the second task?"

"Ah yes, it was reading *Catcher in the Rye*. This task taught me the power of breaking down larger tasks, like reading a book. I remember being surprised at how quickly I finished the book. I also learned that I couldn't do something like reading a book unless it was within my reach. Having the book with me allowed me to seize moments throughout the day to read a page—or more often several pages once I got engrossed."

"Exactly, Josh. This lesson relates somewhat to the first one—taking action is all about starting. Almost anything can be broken down into several small steps. Suppose we're focused on taking action when something comes up and know that almost anything can be broken down into a doable task. In that case, we're much more likely to tackle it. Nothing is beyond our ability to take some action on it. All we need to do is consider the next step, the following physical activity we can take, no matter how small."

"I understand, Mr. Mac. The first two tasks have truly resonated with me."

"That's wonderful news, Josh. Now, let's move on to the third task."

Josh displayed his journal as he replied, "Here it is."

"Great visual representation, Josh. What did you learn from it?"

"I learned that they often disappear without a means to capture thoughts, tasks, and ideas. You gave me this notepad, and now I always have something to jot down in it. I was surprised at how much I filled it in the first week. It's funny. I initially thought I didn't have much to write, but after a few weeks of using it, I can't imagine not having it."

"Could you elaborate on that, Josh?"

"I've come to realize that we constantly have thoughts and opportunities in our lives. If we don't capture them, they evaporate like steam. Now that I have this journal, even if I can't act on them immediately, I've at least captured them for later. Interestingly, it has also freed me from worrying about them. I know they're there, and I can return to them when I need to."

"That's correct, Josh. You now understand the need to act on whatever you need or want to do—any project once it's broken down into manageable tasks, like taking out the trash.

"Now, you have a place where these tasks are always with you, ready for you to act upon. You've experienced the freedom of capturing them.

"OK, Josh, so what is the fourth assignment?"

"This was an excellent assignment. You got me to capture what I had to do or what I thought might be exciting and write down what I wanted in my life."

"Tell me more about that, Josh."

"I learned that it only takes a moment to think about what I want to be true. The more times I returned to my thoughts, the more new thoughts developed, and I discovered more and more was possible."

"By taking some time to think about your ideas and what you wanted to bring forward, you were able to begin seeing them as being real for you."

"Yes, that's it, Mr. Mac."

"So this is the assignment, Josh. Please take a moment and jot down some ideas you want in your life to be true. You can see how to make that happen. The idea, the thought, has a chance to percolate."

"Percolate? What do you mean, Mr. Mac?"

"Yes, percolate Josh. It gives you a chance to let the idea develop. Just as when you brew coffee, within a few moments, it changes state from water and coffee grounds into this wonderful liquid we can drink. Like your ideas, they go from ideas to lines of words on paper to plans and thoughts that get you closer to making them happen."

"That is so true, Mr. Mac. Plus, with what I've already learned, I know how to take those ideas and turn them into action."

"Very good, Josh, very good. Yes, you have learned that lesson well. Are you continuing to do that every day?"

"Yes, Mr. Mac, every day I work on them."

"Perfect, so let's go into your fifth assignment."

"Sure, Mr. Mac. My fifth task was to make my card. I like this one. It focuses me on what I'm going to do today. Josh pulled out his card and showed Mr. Mac with some real pride."

"That is excellent, Josh. It is. What did having the card do for you?"

"You know, Mr. Mac, I didn't think it would do much for me. Was I ever wrong?"

"How so, Josh?"

"I must look at my card one hundred times a day. It served as a map for me. It guides me on the next steps I'm taking towards, as you say, what I want to be true in my life. When you first told me to do it, I didn't know if it would work for me, but it has. I like the idea of knowing what I can do next. For me, it is where all of the other lessons come together."

"It's true, Josh, it does. In a way, it's your chance to put your stamp on your day with honest intention."

"What do you mean by that, Mr. Mac?"

"I mean, Josh, that you are, with genuine intention, making your day your own. Instead of being in reactive mode, now you are in a proactive place."

"Proactive?"

"Yes, proactive. What I mean by that is proactive means you are deciding to act to face any problems, your needs, or things you want to change, and being proactive means thinking about the future and focusing on the things you can control instead of all you cannot."

"Wow, I like that, Mr. Mac. That is what the card has done for me. I don't know. I have a laser beam to focus me on what I want to happen or what might happen. I now have a toolbox to live my life and make what I want to happen."

"That is so well said, Josh. To think, it only takes a moment to make it accurate and focus on the moments of your day."

"Yes, Mr. Mac, I see why you call it the magic of a moment. A quick question, Mr. Mac, Why don't more people live their lives in this proactive way?"

"Good question, Josh. The reality is most people are reacting that they need help finding their way to a proactive way of acting. In a way, what you are learning leads to you proactively creating your life."

"Mr. Mac, I am lucky to be learning all this.

"I need to say 'thank you.'"

"You're welcome, Josh, but you know you're doing the work. I just learned about this, but you're doing it, and that's one of the keys."

"What do you mean by one of the keys, Mr. Mac?"

"During your life, Josh, you'll have so much information and recommendations given to you. The key is continually learning but finding ways to incorporate it into your life."

"That is a great idea, Mr. Mac, and I will."

"Alright, Josh, let's discuss the sixth task. You've done an excellent job understanding and applying the previous assignments and the lessons I intended to impart. Could you share task six with me?"

"Indeed, Mr. Mac. Task six underscored the importance of review. Honestly, I'm astounded by how integral this has become in my life. I didn't anticipate that."

"Elaborate on that, Josh."

"As I mentioned, it has anchored me in ensuring I'm genuinely pursuing my desires. My extensive review has been beneficial as it allows me to sift through everything I've documented and generate ideas for the upcoming week. There's a unique charm in reflecting on the past and anticipating my week during the review. It's a practice I intend to continue for life. It has become a roadmap for my forthcoming week and, ultimately, my life's direction."

"That's splendid, Josh. It aligns perfectly with my intent for you. Now, tell me about the second part of that task."

"As I mentioned earlier, it provided an opportunity to verify that my actions align with what I claim is significant to me. Asking myself what the best use of my time is during the day enabled me to pause and concentrate on the present moment. Adding notes about the day's events and my subsequent steps felt empowering. I felt invincible. It's astounding how a simple question and brief notes can motivate me to keep going."

"Why do you think that happened, Josh?"

"Well, Mr. Mac, it offered me a moment of truth."

"Alright, Josh, you'll need to clarify that for me."

"Of course, Mr. Mac. It's one thing to jot down tasks and claim you'll do something, but reality unfolds in the present moment. It's not about what you say you'll do but what you accomplish that matters and holds power.

That's how I perceive this task. It has generated numerous opportunities to check if I was true to my aspirations."

"Indeed, Josh. That's what I hoped it would accomplish for you. It enables you to lead a life of intention rather than reaction."

"Now, I feel in control, which is a beautiful feeling. The idea that I can accomplish anything is exhilarating."

"That's fantastic, Josh. Truly commendable. Your hard work and the impressive outcomes of your efforts are noteworthy. I'm confident you've grasped these crucial concepts of the magic of a moment. Are you ready to learn about your final task?"

"Mr. Mac. I'm prepared. Let's proceed."

"Alright, Josh, here it is. Recall our earlier discussion about Kaizen."

"I remember Mr. Mac. Kaizen pertains to making minor alterations in life or executing small actionable tasks for improvement. The idea of "making good better" resonated with me—it suggested that anything is achievable if we take small, consistent steps towards it. As you know, Mr. Mac, I like the phrase 'make it true in my life.'"

"I appreciate that too, Josh—quite a lot. So, can I elaborate on some key points to remember when integrating Kaizen into your life?"

"Of course, Mr. Mac. I'm interested in hearing about it, considering my last task focuses on it."

"Josh, you've hit the nail on the head once again with your keen perception. Let's begin with the first principle of Kaizen. Kaizen necessitates a commitment to seeking an aspect of your life that you can enhance or something you desire to be true that currently isn't."

"Mr. Mac, that makes complete sense. Everything I've been learning and implementing is steering me in that direction."

"Indeed, Josh, it is. You now possess a toolbox of techniques to realize this for yourself."

"I can see that, Mr. Mac. Could you elaborate on what you mean by commitment?"

"Certainly, Josh. It's possible to perceive your life's moments as merely surviving through all your responsibilities. This involves responding to life's demands and those you aspire to achieve."

"I see."

"This commitment implies a continuous quest for improvement, not only in your obligations or desires but also in other areas of your life that you might dream of enhancing."

"That's understandable. I can commit to that. Why wouldn't I? I commit to maximizing and improving my life."

"Precisely, Josh. You're enriching your life with a commitment to Kaizen."

"Mr. Mac, my recent review lesson significantly aids this commitment."

"Josh, in your Big Review, as you call it, you're already contemplating what you want to actualize in your life. The true power lies in the daily and midday reviews, where you pause to reflect on your recent actions. In these moments, you can identify opportunities for improvement."

"That makes perfect sense. What else needs to be in place for Kaizen to occur?"

"Josh, the second principle is deliberate thought about those aspects that would enrich your life. It is a commitment to improving and making something more than a single task happen. Josh, how might you apply what you've learned to achieve this?"

"Mr. Mac, I could use my Big Review to identify my focus areas. I could break down larger tasks into smaller, manageable actions from my initial assignments. By consistently performing these actions, I'll compile a list of things necessary for their realization."

"Exactly, Josh. So, you're committed to continuous improvement while examining your life and identifying actions to enrich it."

"I understand, Mr. Mac.

"So, what's the next step?"

"Well, Josh, it's crucial to have a strategy."

"Please clarify that, Mr. Mac."

"Josh, it would help if you dedicated time to contemplating and documenting these small steps. Some will be one-time actions, while others will be recurring until successful. Recall your first assignment, where you immediately completed the task, and the second, where you took action."

"Yes, those are fresh in my memory."

"Excellent, Josh. The same principle applies when dedicating yourself to continuous improvement at the individual task level or for your life."

"That's fascinating, Mr. Mac. How do I consolidate this for this a ssignment?"

"I appreciate your enthusiasm, Josh. Like the previous assignment, I want you to complete two tasks."

"Alright."

"First, review your daily notes and identify three aspects from the upcoming week that you can improve. Please share with me what they are and how you plan to enhance each.

"Does that sound reasonable?"

"Mr. Mac. I can manage that."

"Great, Josh. The second part of the assignment requires more contemplation. I want you to pinpoint something you'd like to be true in your life that currently isn't."

"So, like a goal?"

"Yes, consider it a goal. It might be something you wish to learn or accomplish. Something that you believe would enhance your life. Once you determine it, I was hoping you could share what it is and how you've broken it down into smaller steps to achieve it."

"That's clear, Mr. Mac. I'll complete both assignments. I'm eager to see what I come up with. It's pretty thrilling."

"Indeed, Josh. This assignment and its commitment will help you make the most of your life. I'm confident that you'll excel at it."

"Alright, Mr. Mac, I've got it and will be ready to discuss it next week. I need to leave now. Ricky and I have a couple of yards to tend to this afternoon."

"Good job, Josh. I'm pleased to see that things are still going well for you. I'm excited to hear about your progress next week."

"See you then, Mr. Mac."

24

The Power of Personal Agency

A s their time together was coming to a close, Josh hoped Peter
enjoyed their nostalgic journey.

Peter acknowledged that the journey had given him a deeper
understanding of Josh. Aware of Josh's impending departure, Peter eagerly
asked if there was enough time to discuss the final assignment. He expressed
admiration for how Josh, as a teenager, had persevered through the challenging tasks set by Mr. Mac.

Expressing his gratitude for Peter's kind words, Josh admitted that
while some tasks were difficult, they were also intriguing. This intrigue
kept him engaged and motivated to complete them.

Peter noted the deep level of trust Josh had in Mr. Mac. Josh whole-
heartedly agreed, attributing the positive changes in his life to Mr. Mac's
influence.

Peter thought everyone could have a mentor to guide them through the
magic of a moment concepts, just as Mr. Mac did for Josh. He then said
that to Josh.

Josh concurred with Peter, acknowledging his good fortune.

Peter complimented Josh for recognizing his luck and capitalizing on it, one moment at a time. Josh appreciated Peter's words and then described his last assignment, assuring Peter they had sufficient time to discuss it.

The assignment required Josh to review his daily notes and identify three areas for improvement for the upcoming week. Additionally, he had to choose an aspect of his life that he wished was true but wasn't and then committed to learning or doing it. He could choose anything he wanted to know, develop, have, or anything that could enhance his life.

He then needed to break it down into smaller, actionable steps.

Josh considered this assignment one of his most significant and promised to share his learnings and experiences with Peter.

Peter was intrigued and encouraged Josh to continue. Josh began by describing his early arrival at Mr. Mac's house. Josh knocked on the door since Mr. Mac wasn't in his usual spot on the front porch.

Mr. Mac greeted him with a broad smile and commented on his early arrival.

Josh apologized for his eagerness, but Mr. Mac dismissed it with wisdom from his grandmother: "If you aren't early, you're late."

Josh liked this saying and decided to remember it. Mr. Mac offered Josh a drink and returned shortly with their lemonade, his journal, and another box.

Josh thanked Mr. Mac and said he had used the waiting time to write his grandmother's sayings in his notepad. He also expressed his intention to incorporate this concept into his life.

Mr. Mac was pleased with Josh's initiative and asked about the assignments. Before diving into the details of the assignments, Josh asked if he could share an insight he had gained from doing them.

Mr. Mac encouraged Josh to share this insight. Josh explained how the assignments had changed his life and how this particular assignment felt important enough to commit to for the rest of his life. This commitment was essential for Kaizen to occur.

Mr. Mac urged Josh to elaborate further. Josh shared how reviewing his week and identifying areas for improvement gave him a rush of energy. He felt excited about actively shaping his life and was confident he could realize his desires.

Mr. Mac affirmed Josh's feelings, noting the personal agency that Josh had embraced.

Josh asked Mr. Mac to explain the concept of personal agency. Mr. Mac explained that personal agency and ownership refer to the belief or experience that an individual is the cause of their thoughts and actions. It's like a switch in one's life that makes them realize that if they want something to happen, it's up to them to make it so. This realization leads to individuals owning their thoughts and the consequences that follow.

"Indeed, Josh, in those treasured moments, you discovered that you could be the true architect of your desired life.

"It's not about dissatisfaction with your current life but recognizing that there are always ways to enhance it. That commitment will propel you to undertake actions you may have never considered. When you distill everything, Josh, it comes down to some fundamental lessons you've learned during your assignments. When I think about the power of the magic of a moment, I consider:

- Action is the most crucial step towards success, like how you acted and took out the trash as soon as you thought about it. Simply taking action is incredibly powerful. You must accept that first step. Take that step right where you are in that magical moment.

- Second, take a small action, no matter how minute, like reading a page of a book.

- To steer your life in the direction you want, you must capture your thoughts and goals and advance moment by moment, day by day, week by week, to create the life you desire. Keep your goals visible so you can contemplate them and visualize them because they are all components of the life you wish for."

Mr. Mac's words left Josh in awe. "Wow, Mr. Mac, that sort of brings everything together. Wow."

"Yes, it does, Josh," Mr. Mac agreed, "and that's what I believe you were conveying to me. You arrived at the same realization during this assignment."

"It's so true, Mr. Mac, so true," Josh affirmed.

"Alright, Josh," Mr. Mac prompted, "I know you understand, but tell me about your last assignment. It seems it was important to you."

"Well, Mr. Mac," Josh began, "as you know, I was given two assignments. The first was straightforward but crucial to me."

"Tell me about that, Josh," Mr. Mac encouraged.

"You asked me to find three things from my notes that took place and identify something I could do to improve them."

"And how did that go?" Mr. Mac inquired.

"Well, at first, I thought it would be easy," Josh admitted.

"Was it?" Mr. Mac asked.

"No, it wasn't," Josh confessed. "The problem I was having was deciding which of the many things I discovered I would choose to change."

"That's great, Josh," Mr. Mac praised him. "It really is. You'll find that many things are so small that you can decide to improve them on the spot or ensure you make the change in the future. Does that make sense?"

"Indeed, it does, Mr. Mac. That's precisely what I did.

"Here's an example of something I changed. Indeed, Mr. Mac, it was my Composition course. I had a paper that I needed to write that was due on Friday. As usual, I procrastinated until late Thursday night. I'm not fond of writing articles."

"Alright, elaborate more."

"As I reflected on the situation, I realized I had never allotted it the right time because I always waited until the last minute. I would write it in one sitting. As a result, I completed it at the last minute and usually could have done better if I had allowed more time. As I pondered this, I felt I needed to be a proficient writer and yet despised doing it and, therefore, didn't give myself time to be the proficient writer I could be.

"So, it's akin to a self-fulfilling prophecy."

"Could you elaborate more on that, Mr. Mac?"

"Yes, a self-fulfilling prophecy. What it signifies, Josh, is simply the physical outcome of a situation being influenced by our thinking, either positively or negatively.

"What's happening to you in this situation?"

"That's spot on, Mr. Mac, it is." He had never heard that term before. "Wow, it is so true. So true."

"It's familiar to many people, Josh. Your insight by identifying this thing to change for the better shows a tendency you have that can be changed."

"It's so true, Mr. Mac, so true."

"Remember this, Josh. Most things in your life can be changed if you take the responsibility to notice them and decide how to improve them. So, what did you choose?"

"Mr. Mac, many magic of a moment concepts and assignments have been about noticing."

"Yes, Josh, it's true. Most people must take the time to see what is right in front of them or what they can do to change those things. You can't change what you don't notice."

"That makes sense, Mr. Mac."

"So tell me, Josh, what did you decide to do about this behavior?"

He thought about a couple of things. "First off, I need to start writing it sooner. Even if it is just a few sentences or ideas; second, I should outline what I want to say; third, I should write from the outline I create and get something done, but it is crucial to do it at least one day before it is due."

"Why is that Josh?"

"Well, that was the fourth change I wanted to make. I wanted to use that day to think about it and make any edits before it's due."

"That sounds like an excellent plan, Josh."

"I think so, too, Mr. Mac. Want to hear a strange thing that has happened because of these changes?"

"Yes, Josh, I would love to hear it."

"Since he decided on these small changes, he found that he was actually looking forward to the next writing assignment. Is that wild or not?"

"No, Josh, it isn't crazy at all. Magic does happen when we take steps to claim our lives and make the most of them.

"When you think about it, the things you say you want to do break down the task and give you quick things you can do to make it happen the way you want, and you are now more assured that you will have success."

"Precisely, Mr. Mac, I do think and feel that. It is so true. It is an empowering way to look at life."

"It is empowering, Josh. Taking personal responsibility for the life you want is so much better than feeling victimized about what is happening in your life. Just think about it: before these insights, you had to write a paper, and now you can write it on your own terms. It is very empowering, and you have become aware of how you approached writing in the past and said no more, I'm going to do it my way."

"It is true, Mr. Mac, totally true."

"So, Josh, tell me about the final assignment on what you want to add to your life."

"Mr. Mac, I don't know if you know this, but no one in my family has ever attended college. My dad started but still needs to finish."

Josh doesn't know much about him, but he knows he didn't finish. He joined the Army.

"I wasn't aware of that, Josh."

"Yeah, I don't know him. My mom never talks about him. Anyway, as I thought about everything I wanted to add to my life, I choose to go to college."

"Even more than getting your car?"

"Yep, if I can go to college, I will find a way to get cars in the future."

"That is a great way to think about it, Josh. Impressive."

So the more he thought about it, the more he realized if he chose college now, it would give him time to figure out what he could do to make it happen.

"Fantastic, Josh. Please tell me some of the things you thought you might do."

"Yes, Mr. Mac, I thought I could schedule an appointment with a guidance counselor at the high school. Second, I kept a small paper pad with notes about what I needed to do to make things happen."

Josh remembers pulling it out of his pocket and being proud to show Mr. Mac.

"Very good, Josh, very good. Did you come up with some other ideas?"

"Did I ever? I started to think about what it would take to prepare for the SAT and anyone I knew who had gone to college.

"I even thought about going to a few local schools and just walking around. Does any of that make sense?"

"It sure does, Josh, it sure does. Let me ask you one question. You said these two assignments had a lot of impact on you. Please tell me more about that."

"Sure, Mr. Mac. I realized that the moments of my life opened up an entire world of opportunities, I mean a globe as a whole."

"That is so true, Josh. You realize in every moment and action you take that you are voting for the person you want to be."

"A vote, Mr. Mac."

"Yes, a vote, Josh. Let me explain a little more. When you begin taking what at times might seem to be insignificant actions, you are affirming to yourself and the world this is what's important to you. You are no longer talking about it.

"You are choosing the person you want to be, like voting for a candidate in an election."

"I didn't think of it like that, Mr. Mac, but I see what you mean. That is why, well, it's changing me."

"Tell me more, Josh."

"I feel a sense of purpose in my life. I'm not just getting through a day. I'm making my life my own, not just reacting to everything. It's making conscious choices about what I want in my life. Does that make sense?"

"It sure does, Josh, and I couldn't be happier for you.

"You've got it. Let me ask you something. Will these lessons stay with you?"

"Yes, Mr. Mac, what I have learned and have personally experienced has changed my life. It has. I wake up every day now expecting to make the day mine. I constantly think about the best use of my time and what is possible in the next moment."

"That is great, Josh. I couldn't be more thrilled for you. I really couldn't. I know our time and assignments have ended, but I look forward to continuing to talk and learn about all you make happen in your world."

"Mr. Mac, you changed my life. Perhaps more than anyone ever has. I am so thankful for you and all you have done for me."

"Josh, can I give you one last thought before we end?"

"Of course, Mr. Mac."

"Let me suggest one other way to use the moments of your day. At the end of every day, take just a moment or two and write down two or three things you are grateful for. Just consider your day and find something that meant a lot to you that you genuinely appreciate."

"I will do that, Mr. Mac. I'll do it."

"I know you will, Josh. I have so much faith in you and expect to see what you do in your life. I have something I would like to give you if that is OK."

"Sure, Mr. Mac, thank you, but I should be giving you something, not you giving me something."

"Well, Josh, you will go far in life, and I wanted to give you something to take along the way."

Mr. Mac reached down by his chair and held a neatly wrapped package for Josh.

"Please, Josh, open it."

Josh opened the package and immediately realized that Mr. Mac had given him a folio just like his.

"Mr. Mac, this is fantastic."

"It is Josh. It will help you along the way. Use it as a tool to make your life magical, one moment at a time."

"I will, Mr. Mac, I will. You mean the world to me."

With a tear in his eye, Josh stood up and said, "I better go," and reached over to hug Mr. Mac before leaving the porch. As he reached the street, he looked over his shoulder and shouted, "See you soon, Mr. Mac, and thank you for everything."

From afar, he observed Mr. Mac nodding his head several times, and he knew that Mr. Mac understood how much he meant to him.

25

The Power of Reflection:
A Legacy in Notes

"**W**ell, Peter, we just got that in," Josh smiled.

"Josh, thank you for sharing this story with me. I can see how transformational it was to you. I know we didn't have much time to talk about Generation One, but to know you and how you got to this place is more important. I do have one more question, Josh, if you have time to answer it," Peter responded.

"Sure, Peter, we have a few minutes. As you know, those few minutes allow for a lot of magic," Josh replied.

"Yes, I do, Josh. So, what was it like to get up and leave that day? I know, but I would like to hear it from you," Peter asked.

"Peter, at that particular moment, I was overcome with gratitude and just awe of what Mr. Mac had taught me. As a fourteen, soon-to-be fifteen-year-old boy, I didn't want him to see me get all teary," Josh explained. "So, I left before Mr. Mac could see my tears."

"Did you truly have tears?" Peter inquired.

"Yes, I sure did. If I allowed myself to think about it, I could. As you can imagine, telling you this story has brought back many significant memories," Josh confessed.

"I can see that, Josh. That last lesson really had an impact on you," Peter noted.

"You know it did, Peter. I have developed that habit of looking for ways to improve things, not from a perspective of dissatisfaction but from the knowledge that life offers many opportunities to grow and develop," Josh said.

"You used that with Generation One, didn't you?" Peter asked.

"Yes, even before Generation One, I observed where I worked and believed there was a better way. It has become a way I look at life. I'm always looking for that opportunity to see the good. I have found it is always there if I look for it," Josh replied.

"It really is. I can see that. Did Mr. Mac ever see the success you had?" Peter asked.

"Yes, Peter, he did. He even came to my graduation from college," Josh shared.

"I'm so glad he could do that, and it all started with that last assignment," Peter noted.

"Yes, it did, Peter, the first of many things I have added into my life to make a difference. His lessons are with me always," Josh agreed.

"That was great of him to give you that portfolio. Do you still have it?" Peter asked.

"I sure do. Here it is," Josh said as he lifted it and showed it to him.

"Is that the same one?" Peter asked in sheer astonishment.

"It sure is. I have used it every day of my life since then. I can't tell you how many pads of notes have been written on it," Josh confirmed.

"You still use it even in this time of so much being digital," Peter observed.

"I sure do. Of course, I use some digital tools. You almost have to. I find that capturing my thoughts and thinking through what I want to do happens best on paper for me," Josh explained.

"That is fantastic, Josh. Really, it is. Do you keep all of those old notes?" Peter asked.

"I sure do, Peter. They are still with me. Quite a collection by now. It has been a roadmap of my life to date and what I hope to do in the future," Josh shared.

"Exceptional, Josh," Peter complimented.

"Well, I know it's time for you to go and prepare for your speech. I want to write down a few notes from our conversation," Peter said.

"That's a great idea, Peter. If you would like to speak again, let me know. I will make it happen. We can talk more about the company in a future conversation. Thank you for listening and allowing me to share something significant to me," Josh offered.

"You know, Josh, you should consider putting this all down on paper. As a book, it would be something people would benefit from," Peter suggested.

"You know Peter, during this conversation, that came to me as well. It should be something shared. Everyone deserves the opportunity to have the magic of a moment," Josh agreed.

"I know I would buy the book, and I would certainly make sure my children had a chance to read it," Peter assured.

"Thank you for the encouragement, Peter. OK, I better go. Please feel free to use this room as long as you wish. I have a seat reserved for you in the front of the auditorium," Josh said.

"That is very kind, Josh, very kind. I will see you in a bit. Good luck with the presentation. I can't wait to hear it," Peter wished.

"Thank you, Peter. Let's make it happen. Very best, talk again soon," Josh concluded.

26

An Unexpected Encounter: The Magic of Moments

The auditorium was bustling with activity and motion as attendees streamed in and settled into their seats. The expansive hall would soon be filled to capacity as the presentation was about to commence. Anticipation regarding the impending announcement was palpable.

Peter went down the left aisle to find the seat Josh had reserved for him in the front row. He noticed several city dignitaries and some young men and women. He wondered if they were Josh's employees. In addition, there was a very elderly gentleman seated next to his seat. The man sat quietly with a folio in his lap, waiting for the program to begin. Peter speculated he might be a professor or a campus leader.

Realizing that time was approaching, Peter quickly took his seat and exchanged pleasantries with his seatmate.

The man asked, "Are you a friend of Josh?"

"I'm a reporter for the *Wall Street Journal*," Peter replied. "I just met Josh today. He is a very interesting man."

"What an exciting job being a reporter must be," the man responded. "I'm sure you enjoyed your conversation with Josh.

He is a fascinating person and leads a very full life."

"That he does," agreed Peter. "He has accomplished so much and yet was so generous with his time today. He's someone I'd like to know better."

"Well, I have known Josh for a long time," the man said. "I'm sure he'd be willing to make more time for you."

"Nice to meet you," Peter said, introducing himself.

"Nice to meet you, Peter," the man replied. "My name is Mac."

Peter's curiosity piqued at the familiar name. "Mac, you say you've known Josh for a long time?"

"Yes, Peter, for a very long time," Mac confirmed. "I knew him when he was a young boy. We lived on the same street in Florida."

"Earlier today, during our interview, Josh spoke of you," Peter revealed. "He credits you with much of his success and his approach to life."

Mac sat back and smiled at this revelation, his eyes watering as he composed himself. "You know, Peter," he said, visibly moved, "I'm humbled by his comments. It was so kind of him to speak of me. Josh is an extraordinary young man who embraces every moment. I'm proud of him."

Peter assured Mac that Josh had been clear about how his guidance had shaped him into the man he had become.

Mac's eyes sparkled as he sat up straighter. "We started our relationship with a series of lessons about seizing life's moments," he explained. "The truth is he did the work and has continued to apply those concepts."

Their conversation continued, touching on the importance of intentionality in life, the equitable distribution of time, and the value of every moment. Mac shared an anecdote about gold dust from a book he'd read years ago, illustrating how successful people use every moment, no matter how small.

As the lights began to dim for the presentation, Peter thanked Mac for the enlightening conversation. He expressed his newfound understanding of the profound impact of the magic of life's moments.

Mac, in turn, thanked Peter for the conversation and offered his contact information for future questions or discussions. He smiled at Peter's determination to apply these lessons, emphasizing the key to success: the intentional use of life's moments.

27

An Abundance of Gratitude...

Dear reader, you have such a wealth of opportunities to make your life memorable. The one thing you can count on is that there will be many opportunities, literally every moment, to do something with this amazing life. In the darkest and brightest moments, you can live an incredible life. The choices are virtually endless if your mindset is one to take advantage of your moments and make them unique.

What will you do with your moments? Will you embrace them and draw everything you can from them? Will you find ways to live this next moment and the next to the fullest?

I hope that you will take some time at the end of every day to be grateful for all you could accomplish and for those who guided you on your way. Your life is influenced by numerous individuals around you, some overtly and others more subtly. The world before you holds countless possibilities, yet you can only discover them by embracing them. This very moment, right in front of you, is singular and distinct. Understand, truly grasp, that it is within your reach.

May your life be full of Magic moments.

Magic of a Moment Resources

1. Engaging with Gary is a joyful opportunity to learn from a mentor who can inspire you to engage with life's countless opportunities. Don't miss the chance to enrich your perspective—connect with Gary and unlock magic moments today! www.garyfretwell.com

2. Get your copy of *Unlocking the Magic: Your Daily Journal* to help support you each day to embrace the magic of a moment.

About the Author

 Meet Gary, a seasoned professional passionate about personal growth and development. Gary has a wealth of experience and knowledge in motivation, management, organizational change, sales, personal transformation, project management, time management, and more. His dedication to learning is evident in his exploration of nearly one thousand books, training, and programs, making him a true expert in the field.

During his twenty-five years on campus, Gary served as a faculty member, staff member, and administrator, earning recognition from Tulane University with the prestigious Gary L. Fretwell Leadership Award. Beyond academia, he has spent over twenty years as a consultant and leader in higher education, working with institutions across North America, Canada, Europe, and Mexico. Gary's transformative approach and exceptional speaking abilities have made him a sought-after professional in the industry.

When he's not immersed in strategic planning consulting or life coaching, Gary enjoys the serene surroundings of Prescott, Arizona, with his wife and their two beloved golden retrievers. He is actively involved in philanthropic endeavors, serving as president of Prescott Meals on Wheels and Estancia de Prescott HOA boards.

Gary's ability to connect with leaders, analyze data, and drive organizational transformation sets him apart as a valuable resource for institutions and individuals seeking success. His continued contributions to all types of organizations reflect his commitment to making a positive impact in life.

Engaging with Gary is a joyful opportunity to learn from a mentor who can inspire you to engage with life's countless opportunities. Don't miss the chance to enrich your perspective—connect with Gary and unlock magic moments today!

Website:
garyfretwell.com

Email:
fretwellsolutions@gmail.com

Linkedin:
https://www.linkedin.com/in/gary-fretwell-36691b6/

Facebook:
https://www.facebook.com/gfretwell/

X:
https://x.com/fretwgl

Full Reviews

"We've all heard about the benefits of jotting ideas in a notebook. Still, before reading The Magic of a Moment, *I often found daily writing tedious, limited to tracking to-dos or recording fleeting thoughts. This book changed everything. It introduced me to a simple, actionable roadmap for turning daily writing and reflection into a powerful tool for achieving my goal of living a more purposeful, intentional life.*

The beauty of The Magic of a Moment *lies in its simplicity. The author strips away the intimidating aspects of journaling and replaces them with easy-to-implement daily practices that guide you toward greater self-awareness and growth. What truly sets this book apart is its perspective on continuous growth. It goes beyond surface-level productivity tips, encouraging readers to view each moment as an opportunity to learn and evolve. Reading this book felt like a refreshing reminder that nothing is out of reach. This book is a must-read if you're ready to turn your moments into meaningful progress."*

– Neal Sneller, Executive Director
Prescott Meals on Wheels
https://prescottmealsonwheels.org

***

"Personal productivity and the clarity to live your best, most desired life are skills we all crave. The Magic of a Moment *is a fable that resonates with pre-teens, teens, and adults alike, teaching the essentials of organization, personal productivity, and growth. Readers of all ages will be inspired by Mr. Mac's strategies and his willingness to mentor and celebrate the success of others. I look forward to reading this with my children and grandchildren."*

– Janene Panfil, sister, wife, mom, grandmother,
leader, and a woman striving to live her best life
with her family and friends

***

"I loved this book! At times, Phil Knight, Joe Dispenza, Stephen Covey, and Eckhart Tolle…not copying but pulling from and adding to these ideas in a way that makes personal growth accessible. I'd encourage everyone in my life to read this and apply these seven concepts."

– Eric Groves, Vice President
Liaison International
https://www.liaisonedu.com

***

"The power of The Magic of a Moment *is one of the best tools in your time management/self-help toolbox that a person can begin to utilize! Learning and then implementing the lessons from Mr. Mac at such a young age, Josh becomes a leader in the world of business. Everyone should have opportunity to learn these 'assignments' as early as possible to make the most of the magic in all of their life's moments!"*

– Neal Tessmann, Retired Basketball Coach
Embry-Riddle Aeronautical University
https://erau.edu

***

"This book details a simple and practical way to apply specific tools for turning 'intention' into 'accomplishment' and capturing the value of every moment along the way."

– Robbie Nicol, Retired Healthcare Executive

***

"This book beautifully intertwines life lessons with a heartfelt narrative, drawing readers into the personal experiences of the protagonist. This easy-to-read book provides insights into seven practical concepts that readers can incorporate into their own lives for personal growth and development. The author skillfully blends wisdom into the story, making the lessons comprehensible and meaningful. Enjoyable book to read."

– Marie Larson, Real Estate Agent
https://marielarson.com

***

"Gary Fretwell's book provides relatable characters who, through storytelling, provide us with our call to action, why action is important, the value of trying (even if you are completely unclear on the results), and the strategies needed to execute results. The book explores a story and the power of relationships that connect you with concepts, activities to improve your life and performance, and the value and purpose of daily intentions to achieve results."

**– Dr. Jim Hundrieser, Senior Advisor to the President
National Association of College and University Business Officers**
Nacubo.org

***

"Thoughtful, encouraging, helpful, and kind."

– Richard Ach, Civic Leader and Philanthropist

www.ingramcontent.com/pod-product-compliance
Lightning Source LLC
Chambersburg PA
CBHW060817120626
46557CB00001B/254